WARREN BUFFETT

Master of the Market

WARREN BUFFETT

Master of the Market

JAY STEELE

AVON BOOKS NEW YORK

AVON BOOKS, INC.
1350 Avenue of the Americas
New York, New York 10019

Library of Congress Cataloging in Publication Data:
Steele, Jay.
    Warren Buffett : master of the market / Jay Steele.
        p.   c.m.
    Includes index.
    1. Buffett, Warren.   2. Capitalists and financiers—United States—Biogra-
phy.   3. Stockbrokers—United States—Biography.   I. Title.
HG172.B84S74   1999   99-37729
332.6'092—dc21   CIP

First Avon Books Trade Paperback Printing: December 1999

Printed in the U.S.A.

OPM   10   9   8   7   6   5   4   3   2

We are most grateful to Bruce Cassiday for his creative efforts in helping us to put this book together.

CONTENTS

WARREN BUFFETT

Master of the Market

CHAPTER ONE

The Complete Investor

By the time he was thirty-one years of age, Warren Buffett was already a millionaire.

Twenty-one years later, in 1982, he was ranked Number 82 in the Forbes 400 list of wealthiest Americans. It was his breakthrough year on that list.

By 1983 he had jumped up to Number 31 by doubling his net worth to $520 million.

In 1985 he became a billionaire, worth some $1.07 billion, and was Number 12.

By 1986 he had worked his way up to Number 5 on the list and was included by *U.S. News & World Report* on a list of one hundred people and families who owned the biggest stakes in America's publicly traded companies. There Buffett ranked eighth.

In 1989, with $4.2 billion, Buffett was Number 2 on the Forbes 400 list.

In 1993 Buffett finally reached Number 1, taking Bill Gates's position. With $8.3 billion, he was officially the richest man in America.

Among the most amazing things about this plainspoken, sometimes witty, always sharply intelligent man was the fact that he did it all on his own without a fat inheritance to stake him. He did it by the simple means of investing money in successful companies.

In several other ways Warren Buffett was an unfamiliar figure on the Forbes 400 list. For example, he did not take part directly in Wall Street maneuverings as most of his peers did. Instead, after a certain amount of exposure to Wall Street, he moved back home to Omaha, Nebraska, and from there did all his buying and selling.

For that matter, in physical appearance he did not resemble his peers, either. Nor did he *act* like his competitors on the Street. For whatever reason, he clung tightly to the image of a rather humble, even simple, Midwesterner—homespun, humorous, ever ready with an aphorism to illustrate his point, the Will Rogers of Wall Street.

After so many years of playing the homespun prophet, Warren Buffett had actually *become* that prophet—and it hadn't hurt him one bit.

Honesty and integrity were the two most important elements in the man's character, according to one of his most trusted sources: himself, Warren Buffett. But it was not enough just to *say* that.

In Buffettese it came out this way:

"Never lie under any circumstances. Don't pay any attention to the lawyers. If you start letting lawyers get into the picture, they'll basically tell you, 'Don't say anything.' You'll never get tangled up if you just basically lay it out as you see it."

On the other hand, Buffett was always hedging his more pointed aphorisms just a bit. "Never" became "hardly ever" in this tribute to See's Candy Shops, one of the companies he eventually owned, in which he told how "little white lies" don't always count:

"When business sags, we spread the rumor that our candy acts as an aphrodisiac. Very effective. The rumor, that is; not the candy."

Buffett also believed in loyalty—and expected it of the people with whom he dealt. In Buffett's book, when a friend was hurt, you went to bat for him. One anecdote proved his point.

"I ate lunch at the Omaha Club—that's the downtown club—and I noticed there weren't any Jews. I was told, 'They have their own club.' Now, there are Jewish families that have been in Omaha a hundred years; they have contributed to the community all the time; they have helped build Omaha as much as anybody, and yet they can't join a club that John Jones, the new middle-rank Union Pacific man, joins as soon as he's transferred here. That is hardly *fair*.

"So I joined the Jewish Club: it took me four months. They were a little put back and confused, and I had to do some convincing. Then I went back to the Omaha Club and told them that the Jewish Club wasn't totally Jewish anymore. I got two or three of the Jewish members to apply to the Omaha Club. Now we've got the thing cracked."

Buffett always was upbeat about his work—that is, about investing his money. Did he like his work because it accumulated mountains of cash for him? Or was it something else? As a boy he had said:

"It's not that I *want* money. It's the fun of making money and watching it grow."

That was the key to Buffett's character: making money. He didn't care about having it around, or spending it. He just loved to make it. Once, he was spending time on the West Coast and went as a tourist to visit San Simeon, the gigantic mansion that William Randolph Hearst had built as a repository for millions of dollars' worth of collectibles from all over the globe. After a long session of sight-seeing with the talkative guide, Buffett finally burst out:

"Don't tell us how he spent it. Tell us how he *made* it!"

For Buffett there's an artistic element to making money, a literal sense of creation.

"When I go to my office every morning, I feel like I'm going to the Sistine Chapel to paint."

He could be comical about money, too.

"[I] enjoy the process far more than the proceeds, though [I] have learned to live with those also."

And, to cap it off, he did it his way.

"My guess is that if Ted Williams was getting the highest salary in baseball and he was hitting .220, he would be unhappy. And if he was getting the lowest salary in baseball and batting .400, he'd be very happy. That's the way I feel about doing this job. Money is a by-product of doing something I like doing extremely well."

Vive le by-product!

Warren Buffett's down-home dietary habits were deeply ingrained in him as a child, and after he grew up, it was obvious that nothing could change them. He quite honestly said:

"My ideas about food and diet were irrevocably formed quite early—the product of a wildly successful party that celebrated my fifth birthday. On that occasion we had hot dogs, hamburgers, soft drinks, popcorn, and ice cream."

About the famous "Dusty Sundae"—a Buffett Special—Hershey's chocolate syrup poured over vanilla ice cream, with a layer of malted milk powder over that, he had this lesson to expound:.

"My caloric consumption produced by this concoction is inconsequential. Assume that your basal metabolism rate is twenty-eight hundred calories per day. Simple arithmetic tells us that you can—indeed you must—consume slightly over 1 million calories per year. In my own case—with a life expectancy of about twenty-five years—this means that, in order to avoid premature death through starvation, I need to eat some twenty-five million calories. Why not get on with it?"

Being a gourmet was the farthest thing from his mind from the start. In New York, where the prize targets for gourmets of every size and shape exist, Buffett would eat with friends at the Stage Deli, where he would inevitably order a "roast beef with mayo on white bread." Once, one of his friends, trying to woo Warren over into the forbidden gourmet gardens, suggested a Japanese steak house.

Buffett: "Why don't we go to Reuben's?"

"We ate there yesterday."

"Right," Buffett rejoined. "You know what you're getting."

"By *that* logic, we'd go there every day!" the astounded gourmet observed.

"Precisely. Why *not* eat there every day?"

Malcolm Forbes once brought a fancy wine to a dinner at Kay Graham's house—a wine bottled the year she was born. He said it cost him a bundle. When the waiter got to Buffett, Buffett put his hand over the glass.

"No thanks," he said with that little elfin grin. "I'll take the cash."

If food was a bore to Buffett, clothes were even less significant. He saw clothes not as enhancements of the personality but as covers of the flesh. And he never tried to hone or re-create his image through fashion. As he frankly admitted:

"One of the things that attracted me to working with securities was the fact that you could live your own life. You don't have to dress for success."

Even though he does sometimes wear Italian-made Zegna suits that sell for about $1,500, you can always be sure that the Buffett you see today will be basically the same Buffett you'll see tomorrow.

Warren Buffett's determination to appear casual

caused him to have numerous battles with people who wondered why he dressed so drably, so Omaha-ian, as it were. He would appear in sneakers—called tennis shoes in those dim and distant days. He would wear a shirt unbuttoned at the neck, with his sleeves rolled up.

And when he climbed into more conventional attire for visits to New York or other big cities, he would look scruffy, to say the least. One journalist even called him on it. But Buffett had a comeback:

"I buy expensive suits. They just look cheap on me."

Recently the Omaha Press Club produced a caricature of Warren Buffett by the artist James Horan. Buffett studied it for a moment. It had caught his own unkempt appearance, and in particular his careless, off-the-rack style of haberdashery. He laughed.

"Almost anything beats looking in the mirror."

Perhaps because he worked his way up from nothing all by himself, Warren Buffett decided after he had become a millionaire many times over not to dump all his gains on his children and members of his family. He once called inherited wealth "food stamps for the rich."

"All these people who think that food stamps are debilitating and lead to a cycle of poverty, they're the same ones who go out and want to leave a ton of money to their kids."

Rumors spread that Buffett had cut his children off with nothing. Buffett saw it differently.

"They've gotten gifts right along, but they're not going to live the life of the superrich. I think they probably feel pretty good about how they've been brought up. They all function well, and they are all independent in that they don't feel obliged to kowtow to me in any way."

Nevertheless, he realized that he might have underestimated his offsprings' tolerance just a mite. He once explained his "food stamp" philosophy to a group of college students, and then concluded:

"My kids will be glad to come and rebut this next week."

Buffett has always believed in starting a career early—just as he did.

"I'd been interested in the stock market from the time I was eleven, when I spent some time watching the market and marking the board at Harris Upham, a New York Stock Exchange firm that was in the same building as my dad's firm, Buffett-Falk & Company."

As for his kids, Buffett must have done something right in bringing them up. Susie married, worked for Century 21 in real estate, and then began raising a family. Howard was an entrepreneur from the start, establishing Buffett Excavating, working for See's Candy Shops in Los Angeles, then returning to Omaha to marry and start a family. Peter was always interested in music, and became a professional musician, playing piano with a fifteen-piece band.

Job satisfaction has always been an important concern for Warren Buffett. He chose to work always with people he liked to work with. He selected his associates carefully. In the long run, his care paid off. He told a reporter once:

"I believe in going to work for businesses you admire and people you admire. Anytime you're around somebody that you're getting something out of and you feel good about the organization, you just have to get a good result. I advise you never to do anything because you think it's miserable now but it's going to be great ten years from now, or because you think 'I've got X dollars now, but I'll have 10X.' If you're not enjoying it today, you're probably not going to enjoy it ten years from now."

Buffett incorporated that advice into a speech he later gave at several colleges around the country. One of the colleges happened to be Harvard. A question came up from the floor:

"Whom should I go to work for?"

Buffett takes up the story:

"I said go to work for whoever you admire the most. I got a call from the dean about two weeks later. He said, 'What are you telling these kids? They're all becoming self-employed.'"

(Harvard Business School in fact had turned Warren Buffett down when he applied for admission in his early years, and he never forgot that slight. Anti-Harvard flak crops up in little asides and comments again and again in his later life. It is always something of an inside joke with him—as many of his sayings are.)

One of the men Buffett came to admire most eventually became his partner in the investment business: Charles T. Munger. The two men contrasted in simple blacks and whites: Buffett was a Democrat, although his own father had been a Republican and had served in the U.S. House of Representatives; Munger was a Republican. Buffett was rejected by Harvard Business School; Munger went through Harvard without even having earned an undergraduate business degree. Buffett would be leaving his money to charitable trusts; Munger gave money to liberal causes.

The two men were different in outlook, too. Buffett liked to say yes. Munger liked to say no. Not that Buffett could not say no—he definitely could. But Buffett used to call Munger the "abominable 'no' man."

Buffett liked to give long answers to complex questions; Munger liked to go for the quick and brusque response.

Buffett: "Charlie is not paid by the word."

Also according to Buffett: "Charlie is rational, very rational. He doesn't have his ego wrapped up in the business the way I do, but he understands it perfectly. Essentially, we have never had an argument, though occasional disagreements."

According to Munger: "[Buffett's] brain is a superbly rational mechanism. And since he's articulate you can see the damn brain working."

And Munger has said gloomily: "One of the reasons Warren is so cheerful is that he doesn't have to remember his lines."

The two of them were naturals together, and the Berkshire Hathaway annual meetings immediately merged Munger in with Buffett to make a twosome that many recall equating with that advertising phenomenon of some years ago, the Bartles & Jaymes commercials on television.

Warren Buffett had always loved the smell of printer's ink in the days when he was young. In fact, he had worked as a newsboy for the *Washington Post*, and later, when he was in college in Nebraska, he had supervised a group of boys who delivered the *Lincoln Journal*.

"Let's face it, newspapers are a hell of a lot more interesting business than, say, making couplers for rail cars. While I don't get involved in the editorial operations of the papers I own, I really enjoy being part of the institutions that help shape society."

Warren had always had great empathy with Katharine Graham, the owner of the *Washington Post*. He became good friends with her over the years. She appointed him to the board of directors, and then reappointed him after a short absence. It was one of his better decisions to purchase a goodly number of shares of the *Post* through Berkshire Hathaway. He once wrote Katharine Graham a kind of thank-you note, as follows:

"Berkshire Hathaway bought its shares in the *Washington Post* in the spring and summer of 1973. The cost of these shares was $10.6 million, and the present [1985] market value is about $140 million. . . . If we had spent this same $10.6 million at the same time in the shares of . . . other [media companies] we now would have either $50 million worth of Dow Jones, $30 million worth of Gannett, $75 million worth of Knight-Ridder, $60 million worth of the *New York Times,* or $40 million of Times Mirror. So, instead of thanks a million, make it thanks anywhere from $65 to $110 million."

Warren's homespun philosophy is laced with truisms that sound better when uttered by someone who has created an image like that of Warren Buffett. One of Berkshire's investments, the *World Book Encyclopedia,* always had difficulty in delivering any kind of decent investment returns, as opposed to the fantastic returns achieved by the Walt Disney Company. Buffett thought he knew the reason why:

"The market will pay you better to entertain than to educate."

And here's Buffett on another fact of life:

"We're not pure economic creatures, and that . . . penalizes our results somewhat, but we prefer to operate that way in life. What's the sense of becoming rich if you're going to have a pattern of operation where you continually discard associations with people you like, admire, and find interesting in order to earn a slightly bigger figure? We like big figures, but not to the exclusion of everything else."

For example, Berkshire invested heavily in Capital Cities/ABC, and Buffett assured its CEO, Tom Murphy, that the investment would be a long-term one, not a quick in-and-out.

"It's like if you have a kid that has problems: it's not something we're going to sell in five years. We're partners in it."

Buffett also said:

"I don't think I would feel good about myself if I went around dumping people after they trusted me."

About his sudden burst of popularity in the past few years, especially after the Salomon crisis that he handled from the top, Buffett was not all that pleased. In fact, he felt that being an icon in the business field was not the be-all and the end-all of anything.

"It's not a plus to get terribly well known. . . . We are not equipped to handle tons of inquiries. We get letters from people all over who want advice on investments. I don't like to be hard-nosed, but there's no way I can do it and get my job done."

There was a kind of finality in a recent comment he made about investment:

"You should invest in a business that even a fool can run, because someday a fool will."

In spite of his fascination with and love for newspapers, Warren noted that dealing with the members of the press was always a risky business, no matter how circumspect you were and no matter how you tried to avoid saying something that could be misinterpreted.

"The tough part about it is that essentially there is no one, virtually with the exception of an assassin, that can do you as much damage as somebody can in the press, if they do something the wrong way. There may be doctors out there who can do you just as much harm, but in that case, you initiate the transaction."

He was asked once why he did not favor working in New York City rather than out in what Wall Street considers the boondocks. He would be closer to the focus of all the attention; he would be more aware of what was happening in the world of finance.

"With enough inside information and a million dollars, you can go broke in a year," Buffett responded.

*   *   *

He has always been upbeat about the job of investing money. It is what he does—and does well. There are reasons, of course.

"I love what I do. I'm involved in a kind of intellectually interesting game that isn't too tough to win, and Berkshire Hathaway is my canvas. I don't try to jump over seven-foot bars; I look around for one-foot bars that I can step over. I work with sensational people, and I do what I want in life. Why shouldn't I? If I'm not in a position to do what I want, who the hell is?"

Although Warren Buffett has become known as possibly the most astute investor of the twentieth century, he does have a habit that sets him apart from other men and women who have made themselves into successful investors. He loves to let his stocks ride and simply make money--or lose money—for him. He once explained why he tended to hang in there:

"One of my quirks is that I like to keep things. The best stock to buy is one you are never going to sell."

Selling any of his favorite stocks has never been his main purpose in investing money.

"It's like dumping your wife when she gets old. With all the money I have, I don't want to live my life to get the last one-tenth of one percent."

CHAPTER TWO

Early Days

Warren Edward Buffett first saw the light of day on August 30, 1930, in Omaha, Nebraska. His father, Howard Buffett, had been an insurance salesman, but had turned his hand to selling securities and stocks and bonds for Union Street Bank. The Buffetts had lived in Omaha since 1869, most of them plying the trade of greengrocer.

It would be difficult to determine where Warren Buffett got his absorbing interest in numbers, along with what most folks came to regard as his photographic memory—but, no matter, it was there within him, for his own private use.

His other interest—that is, in the making of money—was something else again. While his photographic memory and wizardry with numbers were a gift of his genetic makeup, his interest in money grew out of the economic situation into which he had been born—the Great Depression. He might almost have at one time or another uttered Scarlett O'Hara's famous words: "As God is my witness, I'm never going to be hungry again!"

Not that he was ever hungry. But he had an obsession about making enough money to live comfortably—and he had it at an early age.

The Depression was making it hard for everyone to survive economically, and about the time of Warren's birth, the bank where his father sold securities folded, and Howard then opened his own shop—Buffett, Sklenka & Co.—in the same building the bank had used.

Warren and his two sisters—Doris, the oldest sibling, and Roberta, the baby—managed to skimp along as kids generally do. When Warren was only five years old, he operated a chewing gum store on the sidewalk in front of his house, selling Chiclets to people who walked by. Later on, he opened a lemonade stand in front of a friend's house on a much busier street. He was quick to learn the facts of life about successful marketing.

Along about the time Warren began to go to school, his father's prospects started improving, and the family moved from the small house they had been living in to a much larger one.

And yet the Depression had made such a dent in Warren's life that he had to think about it. And in thinking about it, he always moved on to do something about making money.

When he was six, the family spent some summer days at Lake Okoboji in Iowa. Warren saw that there were lots of people around the summer camp area and decided to get a store going. He set up a Coca-Cola stand, selling Coke at five cents a bottle, exactly what it would cost in a store.

Ah, but the point was that *he* bought six-packs at twenty-five cents and made five cents on every six bottles he sold! Even at that age he was able to see the benefits of numbers and their application to making money.

The interesting thing about the Coca-Cola stand was that Warren never drank Coke at all. He preferred Pepsi-Cola. He explained once to a shareholder in one of his stock deals:

"I originally started on the Pepsi because at the time

[about 1936] Pepsi came in twelve-ounce bottles and Coke came in six-ounce bottles, and the price was the same. That was a pretty powerful argument."

He instinctively turned everything he knew toward making himself a profit.

But Warren's mind was on other facets of marketing, too, although he would not have known he was dealing with such concepts. What interested him were the discards from the soda machine at the gas station across the street. After the buyers opened the bottles of soda and drank them, the bottle caps remained as a record of the customer's tastes and desires. What Warren was curious about was: How many Coca-Colas were sold? How many Orange Crushes? How many Green Rivers?

He would pile the caps in a wagon and take them home to store them in the garage, going over his collections at times. He kept up on which brands were selling the most. He had a marketer's instinct for wondering what things were moving.

When Warren was seven years old he caught a strange fever that raged through his body. It did not resemble anything the doctors could diagnose. They did remove his appendix, which seemed somewhat inflamed, but that did not stop the high temperatures. As he lay there in the hospital, with the doctors trying to figure out what to do next, Warren asked for a pencil and paper. He filled a page with a lot of numbers.

The nurse was puzzled. "What are those numbers?" she asked.

"Those numbers represent my future capital," he told her. "I don't have much now, but someday I will and I'll have my picture in the paper."

The thought of all that money in the future seemed to cheer him up—and, magically, the fever broke. No one ever knew what had stricken him.

For an ambitious young man like Warren, there was

always work to be had around the local golf course. He knew that by careful searching he could find golf balls that were almost as good as new—marketable to some of the duffers who wanted to practice their swings. And he would gather his finds together and sell them as good secondhand balls whenever he had a large enough collection of them.

In addition, he could always caddy for the more affluent gentlemen who frequented the course and earn $3 a day. Carrying the clubs was no hardship, and sometimes the more cheerful golfers—especially if they had a good day—might even give him a twenty-five-cent tip at the end of the eighteenth hole.

He was a quick study, and he read everything he could about the stock market—stuff that his father left lying around.

"I was fascinated with anything to do with numbers and money," he later recalled.

He would collect rolls of ticker tape and lay them out on the floor, trying to figure out what the symbols on the paper meant. He would look up everything he was curious about in his father's copy of Standard & Poor's.

In fact, Howard Buffett's brokerage company had become a prosperous one. It moved its offices to the Omaha National Bank Building from its smaller site. The boy would frequently visit his father's office, where he would take in all the activity and the undercurrent of excitement that accompanied buying and selling. His father had a new partner now, a man named Carl Falk, and the firm was known as Buffett & Falk, or simply Buffett-Falk.

Occasionally Warren would visit another brokerage outfit in the same building as his father's office—the Harris Upham company, which was a more crowded and lively place than his father's was. The brokers there liked Warren because he looked up to them and admired what they were doing. Occasionally, when the notion struck them, they would hand him a piece of chalk and let him mark the prices on the huge blackboard.

There was something in Warren's blood that would not allow him to pass up an opportunity to develop and try out his own system of determining which stocks would go up and which stock would go down—and when. First he began to take copious notes on the more dramatic of the stocks. He could see that their ups and downs were important, but he could not figure out why the rises and falls would happen.

So he worked on charts day after day, trying to break the code that he sensed must be lurking there in the background—the code that would determine if an offering would improve or decline in value.

Finally, when he was only eleven years old, he simply had to try out the market himself. With his hard-earned money he bought three shares of Cities Service preferred for himself and three for his sister Doris, putting up $38 a share. Almost immediately the stock fell to $27. He knew what he'd lost in the transaction, yet he kept in there, and watched the numbers day by day.

The suspense was incredible. But Warren was made of stern stuff even then—and so was Doris. Eventually the stock moved up to $40, and at that point, Warren sold, making his first profit in the market. He had weathered a downturn and prospered.

Ironically, Cities Services zoomed up the scale to 200 points shortly thereafter. Warren kicked himself. If only he had had the patience to wait out the stock's rise—he could have made a small fortune!

He determined that the next time he had a chance, he'd hang in there, and see exactly where the stock was headed before he sold out at only a marginal profit. He knew he had to learn to curb his own natural impatience and his desire to make a quick buck every minute.

Warren had realized for some time that the stock market, in its own way, operated very much like the race-track. That is, no one really knew whether a stock—or a horse—would have a good day or a bad day. He became fascinated by the similarity. With a good friend, Bob Russell, he began haunting the Ak-Sar-Ben racetrack nearby. Largely at Warren's insistence, the two boys worked out a formula they thought would help customers select the winning horses by name. They tried out the system themselves, checking it each day for a week or so.

Then they made copies of their list of picks, under the headline "Stable-Boy Selections," and went to the track. They began selling their paper, and people bought it. In some instances, the selections worked. In others, they didn't. But the enterprise was short-lived. It turned out that the two boys didn't have a license for operating a tout sheet and the racetrack people shut them down—or at least shut their enterprise down.

Later on, Warren articulated his views on handicapping the horses and investing in stocks in the following manner:

"There are a lot of similarities between handicapping and investing. There are speed handicappers and class handicappers. The speed handicapper says you try and figure out how fast the horse can run. A class handicapper says a $10,000 horse will beat a $6,000 horse. Ben Graham said, 'Buy any stock cheap and it will work.' That was the speed handicapper. And other people said, 'Buy the best company and it will work.' That's class handicapping."

Warren wondered if people could be handicapped in real life the way horses or stocks and bonds were in order to determine their worth in the eyes of humanity. In church one Sunday, he noticed that the composers and writers of the hymns in the hymnal were given birth and death dates. As a matter of curiosity, he began writing down the lengths of these composers' and writers' lives.

It turned out that the life spans of these Presbyterian hymn-nalists were not at all either long or short, but just about average. And so he decided that their religious calling had not been rewarded with anything tangible in the way of the "good life."

In a small way he continued to invest in stocks when he was a teenager in school. The first lesson he took to heart was the one he had found out for himself: not to take the advice of others at all but to decide on a stock because of his own analysis of the company.

Later on he wrote out his ideas along these lines in a letter to members of the Buffett Partnership in 1965:

"We derive no comfort because important people, vocal people, or great numbers of people agree with us. Nor do we derive comfort if they don't. A public opinion poll is no substitute for thought."

He was a reader at a very young age, but his reading was not confined to *Peter Rabbit* by any means. His favorite book was titled *One Thousand Ways to Make $1,000.* The book was a how-to for the wannabe millionaire. It told all kinds of fanciful stories about how to go into business selling homemade fudge, and opening a business in one's spare time. In fact, the idea of being in business and making money never deserted him.

Warren's friend Bob Russell lived on a street where there was a great deal of automobile traffic. One evening as he sat with Bob and Bob's mother on their front porch looking at the cars whizzing by, Warren suddenly realized that he had thought of the source of a gold mine of money.

"All that traffic," he said to Mrs. Russell. "What a shame you aren't making money from the people going by."

His business fantasies never rested.

The attack on Pearl Harbor on December 7, 1941, and the entry of the United States into the war that had been raging for several years on the continent of Europe did little to change Warren's life—but something that happened in 1942 *did*. That was the year the Republican Party in Nebraska turned to Howard Buffett and asked him to run for Congress. After all, Howard Buffett was a real hater of the New Deal and everything it stood for. And so were a lot of other Nebraskans.

Warren helped his father campaign for the job, but he, along with his father, had little hope that Howard would become a congressman. It simply seemed out of sync with what was happening around the country now that the United States was at war.

"He was such an improbable candidate," Buffett said later, "that neither he nor his opponent took him seriously. On election night, he wrote out his concession statement, went to bed at nine o'clock, and woke up the next morning to find he'd won."

Winning was "the happiest surprise of my life," the new congressman said. Howard's "happiest surprise" was Warren's "unhappiest shock." The housing situation in Washington was desperate: the place was overcrowded with wartime people with no place to live. The Buffetts were forced to rent a house in Fredericksburg, a town in nearby Virginia.

The house stood on a hill sloping down to the Rappahannock river—a beautiful, quiet, almost bucolic scene. Warren loathed it. He loathed everything about Washington, too. He couldn't stomach the change in lifestyle. His father, as a freshman congressman, was staying at a hotel in Washington, and the rest of the family was stuck out in the country.

"I was miserably homesick," Warren said later. "I told my parents I couldn't breathe. I told them not to worry about it, to get themselves a good night's sleep, and I'd just stand up all night."

Warren never did come around to his parents' favorable view of Washington and its environs. Instead, he wrote to his grandfather Ernest Buffett and expounded on his unhappiness at living in Fredericksburg. Ernest wrote back and invited Warren to bunk in with him and Warren's Aunt Alice. Warren could finish the eighth grade in Omaha rather than go to school in Washington.

Once Warren was back in Omaha, his entire personality revived. Both Grandfather Ernest and Aunt Alice liked Warren—Alice because he was bright and forthcoming and Ernest because he was interested in books. Ernest himself was writing a book about the grocery business, with the working title "How to Run a Grocery Store, and a Few Things I Have Learned about Fishing."

School was fine, but Warren liked to work after hours. He got a job at his grandfather's grocery store, Buffett & Son. His grandfather hoped that by working at the grocery store Warren would grow to love it and perhaps get into the grocery business himself someday.

Warren hated the physical aspects of the place. It *smelled* of fruits and vegetables. And his grandfather was a true taskmaster. He put all Warren's muscles to work—lugging crates of all sizes and shapes, moving soda pop from one place to another, stacking the shelves with products.

Yet, paradoxically, Warren liked the store itself. It was quaint. When a customer wanted a can from a top shelf, the clerk would move a sliding ladder to the spot and climb up to get the product. The wooden floors were old and creaky, but there was a nice lived-in feel to the whole place. There were rotating fans in the ceilings.

Ernest Buffett ran the store as if he were Lord Horatio Nelson preparing for the Battle of Trafalgar. He worked his clerks from the moment they entered the store to the moment they escaped his vigilance in the evening. Sometimes Warren would come in a minute late in the morning to find his grandfather standing there in the doorway, his pocket watch held ostentatiously in his hand, and looking crossly at him.

Occasionally Warren would lunch at Carl Falk's place. Falk was Howard's business partner at that time. There Warren would take out one of the investment books from Falk's library and begin reading it while Mrs. Falk made lunch for him. One day she asked him where his great interest in making money came from. Why was the making of money driving him so hard that he was always reading about it?

"It's not that I *want* money," Warren told her. "It's the fun of making money and watching it grow."

Mary Falk shrugged and went about preparing lunch again.

When Warren finished school that year, he had no excuse not to accompany his parents back to Washington for his father's second year in Congress. This time the Buffetts were luckier than before. They moved into a house in Spring Valley, a suburb of Washington. The house was located near Massachusetts Avenue. In back there was nothing but woods.

It was a beautiful spot for a place to live, but Warren rebelled against it because he simply did not like the *atmosphere* of Washington. His parents enrolled him in Alice Deal Junior High School, and even with the lively excitement of getting back to school, Warren did not take to it at all. But there was one thing he did do—instinctively. He got himself a job.

He delivered newspapers—the *Washington Post*. He was as meticulous as ever about his business dealings, and he kept accurate records of every cent he made in delivering the *Post*. He even insisted on paying the taxes, despite his father's offer to pay them for him.

As for his life at school, he was in for an unhappy year. His grades, which hadn't been at all bad before, now sank to abysmal depths. Because his scholarship was down, his teachers took to upbraiding him; they knew he was smarter than his grades now showed.

There was one hitch. When he had enrolled at Alice Deal, he had been forced to skip a grade, and that made him just a bit young for his snooty classmates. And because he was used to dressing a bit independently, he appeared slovenly to his Washington peer group—the oddball. For thirteen-year-old Warren Buffett, this was an unusual and dismaying role.

He delivered his papers and kept his records with great care, but at the end of his first year in Washington, with vacation giving him some time to think, he decided that he had had it with the capital of the country. With a friend, Roger Bell, and another school acquaintance, he did what many a contemporary romantic of his age was already doing—he hit the road to see America firsthand.

There was a golf course in Hershey, Pennsylvania, and Warren knew that the three of them could make a bit of spare change staying there a few days and caddying for the golfers. They hitchhiked the first day and arrived that night in Hershey, where they got a room at the Community Inn.

The authorities of Hershey weren't quite so dumb and unaware as the boys had thought they might be. The police took them into custody for questioning the very next morning, early. Three young boys, no matter how they dressed or how they looked, made up a trio that certainly attracted the attention of the law.

Nevertheless, the three boys were pretty astute with their tongues, and managed to talk their way out of the trouble they had landed themselves in. And in the end they were ignominiously hauled back to Washington.

In spite of the fact that he was embarrassed and upset about the whole business, Warren felt that he had learned a lesson about running away from home. The fun had gone out of the venture immediately when the three of them were being questioned by the police officers, who had plenty of experience dealing with teenagers on the run.

Warren decided it was time for him to settle down. He would even try to make himself fit into the new pattern his folks had devised for him. He'd do it in spite of the fact that he didn't like that pattern at all.

CHAPTER THREE

College Days

The youthful rebellion in which Warren Buffett had indulged by running away from home was, in a way, a turning point in his relationship with his family, especially with his father. Howard Buffett, the congressman, was absolutely livid with rage at this bit of petulant mutiny by his son. Although he was seething, he tried to hold in his anger as he sat down for a talk with Warren.

His main problem was with Warren's grades. He knew the boy had a first-rate mind and hadn't become stupid overnight. What was the matter with him? He said that Warren had better get his grades straightened out or the family would do something about it. The threat was obvious: If Warren didn't get his grades up, he'd have to quit his newspaper delivery job.

Warren found himself in a position he had never been in before. He had made a mistake in going off to Hershey; he knew that now. But he was not so sure he could bring his grades up. The truth was, he was just not interested in schoolwork. He was more interested in *work* work: getting the papers delivered.

And so he took exactly the opposite tack almost anyone else would have taken to handle his problem with his father. He did not cut back on his paper route in order to concentrate more on his studies. Instead, he *expanded* it.

The main competitor of the *Washington Post* in those days was the *Times-Herald*. It was the *Post*'s morning competition. And that was where Warren went to expand his delivery service. He took over delivery of the *Times-Herald* in roughly the same geographical area. Indeed, Warren Buffett managed to *monopolize* the newspapers in his part of the city.

It amused him greatly to have a subscriber of the *Post* suddenly cancel his subscription and call up for the *Times-Herald*. As Warren put it, once that happened, "there was my shining face the next day."

But Warren was not content with expanding his deliveries in only one dimension—that is, with two competing newspapers. He expanded in a new dimension by adding four new routes to his original one. By the time fall had rolled around, he was delivering five hundred newspapers each morning. That meant getting up at about 5:20 in the gray a.m. to race outside to catch the bus to Pennsylvania Avenue and pick up the papers. It was a rough job, but it paid off very well, especially with Warren's ability to maintain accurate records of his earnings and expenses.

To his newspaper business he added the selling of magazine subscriptions. He would keep track of the magazines read by each of his newspaper customers by finding copies in the trash cans and ripping off the address labels, which had the expiration date printed on them. Then he would appear at just the right moment and get a commission on the new subscription.

There were other business wrinkles that Warren worked out as well. People were constantly moving in and out of the busy apartments in wartime Washington. In order not to be stiffed by a customer who moved without paying, Warren gave a free paper to the elevator operators for letting him know when a customer was departing so that he could collect beforehand.

He was already a full-fledged businessman. Maintaining his paper route while he was going to school meant he was pulling down $175 a month, just about the average salary of a young man in any kind of business. He was fourteen years old when he paid $1,200 out of his profits for forty acres of Nebraska farmland. He did not feel at all like a member of the landed gentry. But owning that farmland made him feel a whole lot better about himself and his prospects for the future.

He was now attending Woodrow Wilson High. His success with his paper routes and other business ventures gave him a self-confidence that he had lacked before. He felt that he had a pretty good idea of what he wanted to do in life after he got out of school.

In high school he seemed to attract a number of friends with his never-flagging interest in money matters. He got together a group of his peers and they went out and hunted golf balls to sell to the local golfers. In the process he became a pretty good golfer. At least he was good enough to be on the high school golf team.

Donald Danly was the son of a Justice Department attorney—and was a brilliant student. His main interest in life was science, but he was also a very good mechanic. He and Warren began hanging around together and it turned out that Danly, like Warren, had an interest in numbers. Danly was fascinated by Warren's ability to do mathematical problems in his head. He loved to sit and reel off long series of two-digit numbers and wait for Warren to come up with the sums. The two were interested in the odds of numbers—poker hands, or bridge hands, or even the number of people in the same room who might have been born in a particular month of the year.

When Warren was a senior, Danly bought a second-hand pinball machine for $25, and he and Warren spent hours trying to beat one another. When it broke, which was often, Danly would fool around and get it going again. Warren, who had no patience with machinery, was fascinated by Danly's aptitude for mechanics.

Then Warren got a great idea: Why not put the pinball machine to work for them? There were loads of barbershops nearby where they could set one up.

One barber agreed to a fifty-fifty split. At the end of the very first day of operation, the two boys found $14 in the machine. And the amount kept on building. Within a few weeks the boys had three machines in three barbershops. Warren came up with a name for their "company": the Wilson Coin-Operated Machine Company.

"Eventually we were making fifty dollars a week," Warren Buffett later recalled. "I hadn't dreamed life could be so good!"

The company prospered. Warren supplied the money to buy more and more secondhand machines; Danly was there to fix them when they broke. The barbers simply called them up when the machines jammed, and Danly and Warren would appear to fix them.

Warren was not naive about the business he and Danly were in. He knew that there was plenty of danger from the mob, which actually controlled the pinball business all around Washington. So Warren and Danly confined their operations to small barbershops where there wasn't all that much business. And Warren lied just a little. He made it *appear* as if he and Danly were working *for* the mob—and not in direct competition to it.

"The barbershop operators were always pushing us to put in new machines," he recalled, "and we'd always tell them we'd take it up with the boss. We pretended like we were these hired hands that were carrying machines around and counting money."

Meanwhile what Warren considered his "life in exile" continued. His father, who had insisted he wanted to serve only one term in Congress, was reelected in 1944, and again in 1946.

Warren graduated from high school in June 1947, placing sixteenth in a class of 374. His father immediately began advising him on what college to go to. He argued that a good business school like the Wharton School of Finance and Commerce at the University of Pennsylvania might be just the place for Warren.

In fact, that was the very school Danly had selected. So Warren applied and was accepted.

Meanwhile, he and Danly sold out their operation in the coin machines for $1,200 to a returning veteran of World War II; the war was all over in the fall of 1945 and there were hundreds of thousands of veterans looking for work. Warren's paper-delivering days were also over by the time he packed his bags and headed for Philadelphia.

It was not difficult at all for Warren to settle down in the sedate atmosphere of the business school campus. The problem was that he could not seem to find anything of value in the studies. He hated this dreamlike academic world that blurred theory and reality. Instead of discovering new ways to make a hard profit from a business, he found himself listening to and reading over hackneyed lessons in the theory of supply and demand. Well, he already had a pretty good idea of what *that* was!

He was a lot more sociable in college than he had been in high school. He was rushed and pledged Alpha Sigma Phi in his freshman year. During that year he roomed with a friend from Omaha. Soon enough he ran into another freshman who would turn out to be a very good friend.

The young man's name was Jerry Orans. He came from Brooklyn. Warren helped Orans get into the swing of campus life—Orans felt himself to be some kind of

weirdo, coming from Brooklyn and all, thrown in with
all the rest of the hip suburban college kids.

Orans immediately clicked with Warren. He had a
quick wit and a startlingly bright outlook on life. He also
had a good brain—he immediately decided that Warren
was a "genius," and he spread the word around campus.

The first year at Wharton passed quickly. In his sopho-
more year Warren moved into the Alpha Sigma Phi
house. He was amused at the stodginess of the architec-
ture: the house was a Victorian-type mansion with a huge
spiral staircase and lofty ceilings. He was also amused at
the sometimes stiff behavior and "collegiateness" of his
fraternity brothers.

But he fit in nevertheless, much more than he had in
high school. After lunch each day he would grab one of
the bridge chairs by a huge bay window and join in a
game of bridge—or hearts, if there weren't any other
bridge aficionados available. When he played cards, he
played to *win*. And he usually did.

Another side of Warren came out during his fraternity
days. In spite of his general aloofness and his natural
silence, he was a born conversationalist. At the fraternity,
with an audience always on hand, he began to emerge
more and more as the funniest guy around, a born
raconteur.

He cultivated a kind of offbeat Midwestern humor—
a style that was a grassroots caricature, actually. His in-
sights were usually couched in homespun words and
phrases that made them that much more pungent and
enjoyable to his city-bred brothers. Within ten minutes he
could get an entire roomful of people over to his chair,
listening raptly to him and exchanging bon mots in rapid-
fire sequence.

And how the aphorisms soared!

His fraternity brothers loved him. He became a kind
of showpiece when there were parties at the house. And

Warren always obliged. He continued to play the part of a performer at a club, rather than "one of the boys."

In 1948, Warren's second year at Wharton, his father was beaten in the election and moved the family back to Omaha. Without saying anything to anybody, Warren decided to return to Omaha, too, to see if his luck would change any. There were no business ventures to hold him to Philadelphia. Only the college. Why not switch colleges as well?

In Warren's words: "I didn't feel I was learning that much. Nebraska called, Wharton repelled." "Nebraska" meant the University of Nebraska.

No one ever tackled the school the way Warren Buffett did. His entire schedule of courses was put together to get him out of there in one year rather than two. He took five courses in the fall of 1949 and six in the spring of 1950. These were courses in economics and in business.

He also took on a newspaper job, supervising paperboys in six rural counties for the *Lincoln Journal*. It paid seventy-five cents an hour for all its intricacies and headaches, and the circulation manager was unsure whether or not Buffett could handle the job. Buffett, however, was definitely excited to make the position a success. It was indeed a man-sized job, as he found out once he had started.

He kept in touch with his friend Jerry Orans, the Brooklynite at Wharton, and this was the way he described the work in a letter:

"If you have a down route in Seward or Pawnee City or Weeping Water, Nebraska, you're looking for a kid to deliver fifteen papers a day or something of the sort and you got to find him late in the afternoon or early in the evening while you're attending college—it's an education."

In the winter of 1950 the restless Warren Buffett plunged once again into his secondhand golf-ball business. This time he worked it with a remote partnership with Jerry Orans. Warren would collect the balls and send them back to Orans in Philadelphia.

"I don't imagine the boys back there are playing much golf yet and I can guarantee March 1st delivery on the type of balls you want so don't hesitate on getting orders."

He delivered a batch of balls to Jerry, and followed up delivery with a letter reminding him that his golf-ball business was not a "charitable venture."

"By this time I imagine you are bathing in luxury with the enormous profits you undoubtedly reaped from the sale of those gleaming beauties I mailed your father's partner in crime. However, don't forget that Philadelphia's prosperity is not shared by Lincoln until you dispatch a check for the token sum of $65.94."

By July Warren had made $1,200 from the 200 dozen golf balls he had sent Jerry.

He was still moving at breakneck speed in his college career. He took three courses during the summer in Omaha, living at home with his parents, in order to finish the program he had enrolled in.

He graduated with a B.S. from the University of Nebraska in 1950, at the startlingly young age of nineteen.

He continued his correspondence with Orans, who had been a grade ahead of him, and was now opting for Columbia Law School. But Warren had other, bigger plans. In a letter to Orans he wrote:

"Egad! Big Jerry, reconsider and join me at Harvard."

Warren did apply for admission to Harvard Business School. He took the train to Chicago, where he was scheduled to meet an alumnus of Harvard Business School who agreed to look him over as a possible candidate.

It was not an auspicious meeting. Warren Buffett was only nineteen years old, and not altogether a polished individual in spite of his high I.Q. In addition, he had never bothered to study his wardrobe the way some college students did. He was exactly what he appeared to be, the image of the Midwestern hick.

The interview was mercifully brief—ten minutes at the outside. Years later Warren commented on it, intimating that everything was against him—especially the image he projected at that time. Not sparing himself at all, he described "a scrawny nineteen-year-old who looked sixteen and had the poise of a twelve-year-old."

In writing to tell Jerry Orans the truth, Warren buried the news deep in his letter.

"Now for the blow," he wrote. "Those stuffed-shirts at Harvard didn't see there [sic] way clear to admit me to their graduate school. They decided 19 was too young to get admitted and advised me to wait a year or two. Therefore I am now faced with the grim realities of life since I start paying room and board here in four weeks. My dad wants me to go on to some graduate school but I'm not too sold on the idea."

In a later letter, he wrote: "To tell you the truth, I was kind of snowed when I heard from Harvard. Presently, I am waiting for an application blank from Columbia. They have a pretty good finance department there, at least they have a couple of hot shots in Graham and Dodd that teach common stock valuation."

Graham and Dodd were far from the "hot shots" that Warren's flip phrase implied. Benjamin Graham had become known as the dean of the securities profession. He and David Dodd had authored a textbook that effectively staked out the field. In addition, Graham had written a second book, *The Intelligent Investor*, which Warren had read—avidly.

Graham was born to Benjamin Grossbaum in London in 1894, but was brought to New York a year later when his father opened a branch of an import business. After excelling at Boys' High in Brooklyn, Benjamin went on to Columbia, graduating in 1914 to enter Wall Street as a broker.

His approach was to spot companies so cheap that they were free from risk. And his approach obviously worked. By 1929 "Benjamin Graham Joint Account" had $2.5 million in capital. Graham was in clover. When the Crash came, the Joint Account lost 20 percent. A relative of Graham's partner, Jerome Newman, put up $75,000 and saved the firm.

Boiled down to three words, Graham's philosophy was "margin of safety." An investor should insist on a big gap between the price he was willing to pay and his estimate of what the stock was *worth*. The real trick was in valuating a company—that is, determining its true worth rather than the worth the company wanted the public to apply to it.

Benjamin Graham had twenty students at Columbia in 1950—one of them Warren Buffett, who turned the lessons into dialogue. Graham introduced his ideas in typical Socratic manner, and Warren had the answer out sometimes before the question was fully phrased.

Graham loved cheap stocks, those that could be picked up almost free. He was a master at explaining to his students how to read financial statements and spot frauds in them. What he was teaching them was the way to extract a fair value from all the gobbledygook that went into the published material the company sent out.

Warren had one favorite maxim of Ben Graham's that he kept always in the back of his mind.

"Ben Graham would say that you're not right or wrong because one thousand people agree with you or disagree with you. You're right because your facts and your reasoning are right."

And he would hold strictly to that maxim throughout his years of investment.

Warren graduated from Columbia in 1951 and decided to get into stocks immediately. He knew that Graham had given him the highest grade he had ever given one of his students at Columbia—an A+—and so he had the best reason in the world to make him an offer he couldn't refuse. He told Graham that he would gladly go to work for Graham-Newman for absolutely no compensation.

Graham said no.

Warren was flabbergasted. He couldn't understand Graham's reasoning. Later, when people asked Warren what he thought caused the Great Man to refuse his prize student, Warren usually turned to a nonserious, joking response.

One such answer was this: "Ben made his customary calculation of value to price and said no."

Another went: "He turned me down as overvalued."

Warren accepted the turndown less than philosophically and turned himself around to go back to Omaha, where he went to work for Buffett-Falk & Company, his father's firm. He worked there from 1951 to 1954. But meanwhile, other things were taking place in the life of Warren Buffett.

Roberta Buffett, Warren's younger sister, was going to Northwestern University at the time, and was rooming with a young woman named Susan Thompson, the daughter of an Omaha minister and psychology professor.

Once he met Susan during the summer of 1951, Warren began going out with her. And he bored Susan to death. His conversations with women usually involved minute trivia, idiotic brain-teasers, or conundrums of one kind or another. As time passed, when he came in the front door, she started going out the back door.

Warren ended up talking to her father, wooing her through him, as it were. The young man was a fair hand with a ukulele. Susan's father had played the mandolin since he was a youth. And so these two made beautiful music together, while Susan slipped out the back door and made beautiful music with a fellow named Milton Brown, a Union Pacific mail handler.

The music finally won the day. With Susan's father constantly reminding her of what a great guy Warren Buffett was, she simply couldn't ignore him totally. And she eventually began going out with him again. Then, to her shock, she discovered that he really did have a sense of humor under that exterior of trivia and off-putting brain-teasers.

They were married in April 1952 at Dundee Presbyterian Church.

Warren Buffett: "It was obvious I was not Number One with her. But [her father] became very pro-me. It was two against one."

In *Buffett: The Making of an American Capitalist*, Roger Lowenstein tells the story of what happened on their wedding night—maybe. As the newlyweds drove west to California on their honeymoon, they stopped at a café outside Omaha for a light meal. On the way to the car Warren noticed a Cadillac parked at the curb of a company headquarters. He got inside the building and talked to the company president while his nineteen-year-old bride waited in the car, fuming.

After all, he just had to talk business with a man he knew was at the top of the heap, at least in one company.

CHAPTER FOUR

The Partnership I

Getting married was an essential step in the life story of Warren Buffett. Yet it was hardly the be-all and end-all of his existence. Nor was it that of his wife's. The newly married Buffetts moved into an inexpensive three-room apartment in Omaha that was in no way the household Susan had envisioned when she agreed to marry him. In the words of the scriptwriters (and the voice of Bette Davis), it was a "dump." But the two young Buffetts settled down without any folderol and started trying to make their marriage work just like so many others in their situation.

Although Warren worked hard at Buffett-Falk, he had other dreams, and he continued to invent little things that might get him into a position that would be better for him than his stint at Buffett-Falk. But all that, of course, would take time.

What he still wanted, of course, was to work for Ben Graham in New York. Graham had been adamant in his refusal, but Warren thought he had a way of convincing Graham of his worth.

"I started trying to be useful to him in various ways,"

Buffett later explained. "I did a number of studies I dreamed up. I tried to suggest ideas."

Buffett equated his actions with those of a football player in a like situation. "If I wanted to be starting quarterback on the Washington Redskins, I'd try to get them to watch me throw a few passes."

But nothing seemed to work, and Warren kept his nose to the grindstone at Buffett-Falk. Aunt Alice was his first customer. He persuaded her to buy one hundred shares of GEICO. GEICO, or Government Employees Insurance Company, was a rather esoteric stock to purchase. They sold automobile insurance by direct mail, usually to government employees. But Benjamin Graham was chairman of the company, and, for Warren, *that* was reason enough to invest in it. Indeed, it was a good stock for his aunt to purchase. Within two years it doubled in value.

But Aunt Alice was not his only customer. He sold to anyone who would buy. He spent most of his time as he had always spent it, slogging through Moody's manuals page by page. And in his hunt he uncovered little jewels of stocks that were unwanted by a public that had never heard of them but that were solid investments going begging. Warren followed Ben Graham's advice here, picking up such oddball offerings as Kansas City Life, Genesee Valley Gas, and Western Insurance Securities. All these were trading at three times their earnings or less.

Warren Buffett was right in grasping these fine little treasures. But in the public's eye, he did not look like a winner. Even when he managed to sell one of those favorite stocks, his commission was smaller than those of the other brokers in the office—because the stock was usually trading for less!

That made his customers chalk him up as a novice. Even those he'd impressed would often go to a more seasoned broker for a second opinion, and if Buffett's advice proved good, then buy the stocks from the old hand.

Meanwhile, his marriage was thriving. On July 30, 1953, a daughter, Susan, was born. The Buffetts were still living in the confines of their tiny stuffy apartment, but somehow wife Susan managed to cope.

Warren kept up his correspondence with Benjamin Graham, sending him tout sheets for stocks he had found in his researches, and discussing Wall Street gyrations with him. Somehow it might pay off, Warren thought. At least he hoped so.

A born moneymaker like Warren Buffett could not keep his hands off a new business venture when it suddenly presented itself to him. And so he bought into a Texaco gasoline station and purchased some acres of real estate to go along with the farmland he already owned. Neither venture worked out, though. Warren sadly closed the curtain on them and turned elsewhere for his next move.

He was getting better on his feet as a salesman, although he did not have a salesman's glib manner of speech or his art of persuasion. In fact, Warren knew he was ineffective in front of a crowd, in spite of the fact that he was excellent in a chair with people all around him—smaller numbers of them, at least.

He invested in a public speaking course run by one of the most famous names in public speaking history, Dale Carnegie. The Carnegie class helped him smooth his speech patterns and taught him how to organize his thoughts before plunging in with an essay of some kind. He finally managed a process where he could come up with a theme, develop it point by point almost instantaneously in his head, and speak to those points in order as he stood there.

After honing his public speaking abilities to a fine edge he got a job teaching a night class, "Investment Principles," at the University of Omaha. This was an era of "ongoing education," and all over the country the middle-aged were mixing in with the younger generation in getting an education.

Most of Warren's students were in their thirties and forties, much older than he, but once he began to speak, they settled down and knew he had something to say that was important. Although most of his lectures were cribbed from Graham's book *The Intelligent Investor*, Warren began to sprinkle little homespun sayings and jokes among the more important tips on playing the stock market.

What those ongoing education students wanted more than anything else were tips on the stock market—specifically, what stock was going to go up and up and up. It got to be amusing to watch the members of his class ask questions about a certain company with a kind of throwaway jauntiness—especially when Warren knew exactly what they wanted to know about the stock. Buy it? Pass it up?

He'd always let them down gently, but he never gave them the slightest hint. He figured he had come by the information about the companies the hard way and it was going to remain in his head and in his head alone, where no one else could get at it—until after he acted on the stock.

Not only did Warren tell his class not to ask anyone else about stocks, but he warned them not to take any advice others might give them on a stock—especially if the others were brokers. The fact was that brokers were usually wrong; they would be touting a stock by the time it had already become popular and was ready to slow down, hit a plateau, or even go zooming down instead of up.

Warren's father had retired from Congress in 1952. In 1954 Senator Hugh Butler died and Howard Buffett decided to try for the nomination. But the moderate Republican cut him down: Roman Hruska was nominated instead.

It was a bad year for Howard but a good year for Warren. Shortly after Howard lost the nomination, Warren got a telephone call from New York. It was Benjamin Graham. He offered Warren a job with Graham-Newman. Warren didn't even bother to ask "how much?" He was on the next plane out of Omaha.

It turned out that Graham would be paying Warren $12,000 a year; Warren was happy with that. He rented a garden apartment in suburban White Plains and commuted every day on the New York, New Haven, and Hartford. It was in White Plains that the Buffetts' first son, Howard Graham, was born, shortly after they arrived in New York.

The office was not in the Wall Street area. It was located on Forty-second Street, right across the way from Grand Central Station, where Warren arrived each morning on the train. The money was good; the stock market was thriving; everything should have been hunky-dory.

And yet there was restraint in the air. All was not completely well in the world of money. The Street was still in the command of men who had gone through the 1929 debacle. The market was at 380 and the old men remembered what had happened when it got high before. They were scared. Graham had been there. He could *feel* the angst in the air.

Mutual funds were all the rage in the years after World War II, and Graham-Newman was a mutual fund. The good thing about mutuals was that the good investments neutralized the bad ones so that the result was usually always some kind of a plus. But the all-important search for good companies to purchase stock in persisted, and Graham had not changed his ideas one bit since his days of teaching at Columbia.

Warren knew how to please Graham. He'd hunt for

stocks that traded at one-third less than their net working capital per share. Net working capital was the total of current assets such as cash, inventory, and receivables, not including plant and equipment, after deducting *all* liabilities. This was right up Warren's alley. He loved to uncover stocks that were "almost insanely on the cheap."

The first year there he brought off a brilliant ploy. He had discovered Rockwood & Company, a Brooklyn chocolate concern, which offered to redeem some of its stock in exchange for cocoa beans, of which it had a large inventory. Warren deduced that trading the stock for beans and simultaneously selling beans on the commodities market—where the price had soared—would produce a huge profit.

Buffett: "For several weeks I busily bought shares, sold beans, and made periodic stops at Schroeder Trust to exchange stock certificates for warehouse receipts. The profits were good and my only expense was subway tokens."

He was dealing in arbitrage, that is, taking advantage of price discrepancies in separate markets. He was way ahead of his peers, as usual.

As for stocks that were "almost insanely on the cheap," Warren found a block of Union Street Railway of New Bedford, Massachusetts, trading at 45, that had $120 a share in cash assets alone. Graham was reluctant, unconvinced that it would work out. Warren bought it for his own account, and it turned out fine for him. He often cited it as one of the "less than one-third" cheapies he had made money on.

Another time, an obscure insurance stock known as Home Protective was offered by a Philadelphia broker at 15 a share. There was nothing written up about the company. Warren went to the state insurance office, in Harrisburg, and dug up the facts. Home Protective was a steal. Yet Jerry Newman, a far less pleasant man than Graham, rejected it. Warren bought it for his own account. Home Protective went up to 70 soon afterward. Warren had been right again.

Working with Graham was a different thing from taking classes from him, Warren discovered. He had thought they would be in and out of each other's office all the time. It was not to be. As Buffett wrote later, Graham "had this kind of shell around him. Everybody liked him. Everybody admired him [and] enjoyed being around him . . . but nobody got close."

In the long run, Warren found it was also a different thing to work for Graham at Graham-Newman than he had anticipated. The mutual fund had only $5 million in capital, and he felt that there wasn't any leeway for making investments. He wanted to invest in stocks and make money grow.

There was also a private fund—Newman & Graham—but that too was small potatoes. In all, the company managed only $12 million. To Warren, it seemed that the two partners were really sitting on the money rather than getting it ready to invest and work for them.

"It didn't seem like much of a life," Buffett told a newspaper reporter later. "People kept coming up to me all the time, whispering into my ear about some wonderful business. I was getting excited all the time. I was a wonderful customer for the brokerages. Trouble was, everyone else was, too."

The frustration ate at him. He could stomach the commute every day from Westchester County to Forty-second Street, but he couldn't stomach the lack of business activity.

Benjamin Graham's fear of another crash like the 1929 one never left him, and finally, in 1956, he moved to Beverly Hills and began teaching at the University of California at Los Angeles. His whole life changed. He began writing for the financial journals, along with preparing lectures for the classroom.

His personal life became a checkered thing. He had always had a roving eye, and mistresses were all a part of his general schema. Now, in Beverly Hills, he lived with his wife and his French mistress. He spent lavishly, declaring that anyone who died with more than a million dollars in his possession was a damned fool.

It was time for Warren too to decide what to do with the rest of his life.

While working for Graham-Newman, he had invested on his own, and had actually done better than the company. He had pushed his own personal fortune from $9,800 to $140,000 in a relatively short time.

He now had a kitty to work with—and he wanted to do something big with it. Anyone who knew Warren could have guessed what he was going to do next. He had made the same move many times before in his life.

He packed up his family and moved back to Omaha.

The Warren Buffetts arrived there on May 1, 1956, and rented a house to live in temporarily while Warren shopped around for a place to buy. The rented house was on Underwood Avenue, not far from the Buffett grocery store.

Warren Buffett's first move was a rather strange one, but one that foreshadowed others yet to come. He pooled money from friends and relatives and founded a thing called Buffett Associates, Ltd.

He said: "I'll run it like I run my own money, and I'll take part of the losses and part of the profits. And I won't tell you what I'm doing."

And that was exactly the way he worked it. The people he was using to form this "partnership" were Charles E. Peterson, Jr. and his wife, Elizabeth; Doris B. Wood, Buffett's sister; Truman S. Wood, Buffett's brother-in-law; Daniel J. Monen, Jr., a friend in Omaha; William H.

Thompson, Buffett's father-in-law; and Alice R. Buffett, Buffett's aunt.

Later he recalled: "I told them, 'What I'll do is form a partnership where I'll manage the portfolio and have my money in there with you. I'll guarantee you a six percent return, and I get twenty-five percent of all profits after that. And I won't tell you what we own because that's distracting. All I want to do is hand in a scorecard when I come off the golf course. I don't want you following me around and watching me shank a three-iron on this hole and leave a putt short on the next one.' "

Here are the numbers according to the limited partnership filed at the Douglas County Courthouse in Omaha in 1956:

Charles E. Peterson, Jr.	$5,000
Elizabeth B. Peterson	$25,000
Doris B. Wood	$5,000
Truman S. Wood	$5,000
Daniel J. Monen, Jr.	$5,000
William H. Thompson	$25,000
Alice R. Buffett	$35,000

Warren Buffett, called a "general partner," chipped in $100 for the paperwork, and would put in more money later on. He would be receiving 25 percent of all the profits above 6 percent annually, with deficits carried forward.

The partnership got off to the kind of start Warren Buffett preferred to any other kind: a quiet one, one in which he was not bothered by nervous shareholders, one that he had complete control over, and one that he knew would work out in the long run even if there were short periods of losses.

But his early success was not quite so quiet as he had hoped it to be. A friend of Ben Graham's—a physics professor from Vermont named Homer Dodge—had heard about Buffett and drove all the way to Omaha to meet him in the summer of 1956.

Buffett recalled the meeting clearly.

"Homer told me, 'I'd like you to handle my money.' I said, 'The only thing I'm doing is a partnership with my family.' He said, 'Well, I'd like one with you.' So I set one up with Homer, his wife, children, and grand-children."

Dodge gave Buffett $100,000. And he played Warren's game to a T, keeping his nose strictly out of the day-to-day work of the partnership. In the end, his trust in Buffett proved out. By 1983, when Dodge died, the sum of $100,000 had ballooned into tens of millions of dollars. Dodge had sensed from the beginning that Warren Buffett was a brilliant analyst. In addition, he happened to be a lucky man when it counted most.

Others heard of Buffett's partnerships and some of them tried to get aboard. An entrepreneur named Laurence Tisch, who would eventually become chairman of Loews and CBS, gave Buffett $300,000 along with a brief note.

The note read: "Include me in."

Later, Tisch was ecstatic about Buffett's prowess in the market. He called him "the greatest investor of his generation."

In 1957 Buffett was visited by a well-known Omaha urologist named Edwin Davis. Davis had heard about him from a patient, a New York investment advisor. He wanted to see what kind of man he would be putting in charge of his money.

His first impressions were bad—very bad. Initially, Buffett struck Davis as being "about eighteen years old." He wore his hair too short to fit the fashion of the time, and he didn't even wear a tie. Besides that, his clothes didn't fit him—they were way too big. He talked too fast for a normal person. Most fast-talkers were using their rapid speech to cover up deficiencies in their arguments, Davis knew, and he was immediately wary.

Buffett gave Davis all the usual warnings: he was open for business only one day a year, on December 31, and he would have no contact with Davis at any other time. Except for December 31, when Davis could take out his money or add more, his money would be completely in Warren Buffett's hands to do with as he pleased.

The terms were these: The Davises—members of his family were included—would be limited partners. They would receive all the profits up to 4 percent. After 4 percent, Buffett and the Davises would share the remaining profits: 75 percent to the Davises and 25 percent to Warren Buffett.

The key point in Buffett's partnership plan was the fact that his money was on the line as well as the Davises'. If things went bad, he would end up with zero, too.

In spite of his initial reserve, Davis found that he did like the idea from the word go. Everything was all laid out and clear from beginning to end.

"We liked that. You know where you stood with him."

In the end, Davis put up $100,000 for his family and joined in Warren Buffett's partnership.

By the end of the year, Buffett was working five small partnerships, very much like his original family partnership, and watching the results. In his first year, his partnerships, totaling about $500,000, gained 10.4 percent. That beat out the Dow industrials by about 18 percent, the Dow having suffered an 8.4 percent loss.

Not a bad finale to a relatively fresh kind of investment procedure. Not bad at all for Warren Buffett.

CHAPTER FIVE

The Partnership II

Susan Buffett was expecting for the third time when Warren finally decided to move into more commodious living quarters. For $31,500 he bought a larger house, on Farnam Street, and there the family settled into a more comfortable environment. But Warren still kept his office in the house, managing his partnerships from there.

He had resumed teaching his course on investment at the university. He also established a few more stockholding partnerships that were similar to the Buffett Associates of 1956 that had started him on his way.

Warren Buffett, the man, seemed to expand in Omaha. He had sampled life in the big city and had not particularly taken to it. While in no way a loner, he felt closer to people in the more relaxed environment of Omaha than he did in the bustling, ripsnorting, concrete-and-glass canyons of New York City.

He could think better in Nebraska because those with whom he had daily contact laid little stress on him. He could relax and move easily through his voluminous research projects. He had acquired a desire to know everything there was to know about all the stocks that were on the market at the time. And he was very close to achieving full knowledge.

"I think it's a saner existence here," he told a *New York Times Magazine* writer some years later. "I used to feel when I worked back in New York that there were more stimuli just hitting me all the time, and if you've got the normal amount of adrenaline, you start responding to them. It may lead to crazy behavior after a while. It's much easier to think here."

He was never a very outreaching person, never the glad-handing jokester who was the life of the party. At a gathering, he would sit quietly in a chair, while Susan, his wife, would immediately establish solid contact with anyone new. And in so doing, she would pave the way for Warren's eventual association with that person.

The two of them worked so well in tandem because they were such definite opposites. She was the welcomer, the openhearted one. He was the introverted, intellectualizing type.

After being charmed by Susan, the newcomer might notice that people were circulating around a chair in which Warren Buffett had plunked himself down many minutes before and from which he was now holding forth. For this was the reincarnation of the Warren Buffett who had so energized his fraternity brothers at Wharton. This was the homespun, wisecracking, philosophical guy who strewed his extremely particular speech with sparkling little gems of grassroots wit.

And Buffett had every reason to be bright and happy about his lot in life. Things were going very well for him in the investment business. By 1961 it was obvious that he had done all the right things at exactly the right times. After the astonishing success of his first year—10.4 percent up from 1956, with the Dow sinking 8.4 percent—his next year was another resounding success. In 1958 his holdings advanced by 40.9 percent. The Dow was going up, too, but he outstripped that venerable index by 2.4 percentage points.

In 1959, things were more or less back to normal. His partnerships advanced 25.9 percent, to the Dow's 19.9 percent rise. In 1960 his holdings rose 22.8 percent, while the Dow sank 6.3 percent. In 1961 he again pressed all the right buttons, with his holdings rising at the unheard-of rate of 45.9 percent—almost half again as much. The Dow rose only 22.2 that same year.

In five years the Buffett partnerships had advanced 251 percent; the Dow had risen by 74.3 percent. As the Dow went up three-quarters, Warren Buffett's partnerships went up two and a half times.

Plus, in 1961, Warren Buffett became a genuine millionaire. It was the breakthrough that he had always known would come. Yet it came earlier than even he had anticipated. He was only thirty-one years old.

What suited him fine was the fact that a millionaire didn't have to *look* the part. For Buffett did not look the part, at least according to one of his "partners," quoted in the *Omaha World-Herald.* The stockholder was explaining to the world how you had to navigate a very special route to get to see Warren Buffett at all. And it was hardly the kind of route one might expect.

"You went in the back door of his home," the stockholder said, "walked through the kitchen, the living room, and went up the stairs to the bedroom. If you were impressed with show and image, Warren was not your man. He always dressed like he got his clothes out of a grab bag."

Warren Buffett had never changed his ideas about clothes at all. The fact that he had not done so was in itself a statement to his followers. He continued to wear sneakers—tennis shoes—just like any other hick might. He was a one-and-only: a millionaire in poor-boy shoes.

He could indulge himself now. Not that he *wanted* to.

He was a man who surrendered to few temptations of ostentation. But he did allow himself at least two personal indulgences. He still lugged bottles of Pepsi-Cola around with him in case he got thirsty. And he still loved to play bridge. In fact, his bridge playing was more an obsession than his stock market trading.

According to those who played with him, he was 100 percent focused on the deck of cards during a bridge game—or a poker game, for that matter. And those who watched could see him calculating the cards one by one for each of his companions as they bid during the game. He displayed all the signs of a computer turned on full blast, ticking off every point he wanted to analyze.

William O'Connor, an Omaha man who was working for IBM at the time, met Warren Buffett and became a member of the Buffett fan club. In his book *Warren Buffett: The Good Guy of Wall Street*, Andrew Kilpatrick quotes O'Connor as follows:

"Warren really is a very uncomplicated person," O'Connor said. "He's a super nice guy who just keeps things simple. . . . He has an insatiable thirst for knowledge. He reads from all sources and he has a photographic memory that helps him recall and reconstruct things in an orderly, logical fashion. . . . He plays a little tennis and golf, and I really think he'd rather read—and play bridge—than anything."

It was in 1959 that Buffett met Charles Munger, a man who would be very closely associated with him as a partner for the rest of his investment days. Munger was six years older than Buffett, and had grown up in Omaha, only to go to Harvard Law School and wind up practicing law in Los Angeles. They met because one of Buffett's investors thought that the two of them might like one another. The investor invited them both to the Omaha Club, where they did indeed strike up a quick relationship.

MUNGER: Warren, what's your racket?

BUFFETT: Well, we have a partnership.

MUNGER: Maybe I could do that out in Los Angeles.

BUFFETT: Yeah, I think you could.

Their humor seemed to run in parallel channels. Munger shared Buffett's snobbishness and judgmental attitude, as well as his strong sense of ethics. But he also had a wide-open sense of humor. Asked once if he could play the piano, Munger responded with an old vaudeville saw:

"I don't know. I never tried."

Susan Buffett knew a real friendship when she saw it blossoming in front of her eyes. She could hardly separate the two men when they got together for a chat. They talked for hours, half the time in unfinished phrases or elliptical comments. No use repeating what the other already knew. It developed into a kind of private code almost.

In 1962, Warren Buffett merged all his partnerships into one, calling it the Buffett Partnership, Ltd. He decided at the same time that he had outgrown the house in which he lived—at least in a business sense—and he opened a business office in Kiewit Plaza, on Farnam Street in downtown Omaha.

In his conversations with Munger, Buffett kept insisting that Munger had no business practicing law when he should be in investments. Munger was far from disagreeing with Buffett. He thought so himself and began looking around for somewhere to begin.

Meanwhile Buffett was becoming more and more Warren Buffett in everything he did. His homespun humor was his greatest asset, particularly in the investment game, and he knew it. He began to pepper his annual reports—"Letters to the Partners"—with some of his interesting observations on the investment business. Or on life itself, for that matter.

For example, when he moved his business from the house to the office in Kiewit Plaza, he mentioned the fact in his next letter to the partners. He said that he had left the original so-called office just off his bedroom "to one a bit (quite a bit) more conventional. Surprising as it may seem, the return to a time clock has not been unpleasant. As a matter of fact, I enjoy not keeping track of everything on the backs of envelopes."

Sometimes, as a matter of fact, Buffett simply spun out his letters with a little pseudohistorical nonsense that made the investment business seem just a bit more interesting to his stockholders. To illustrate the "joys of compounding" he estimated that the total cost of underwriting Columbus's voyage would have been about $30,000 in 1492, and then he showed how $30,000 compounded at 4 percent would come to about $2,000,000,000, or $2 trillion, by 1962—a tidy sum indeed that showed the value of compounding interest at an acceptable rate.

But much of the material in the letters was directed to the stockholders in a more serious manner. In the following excerpt, Warren Buffett is talking directly to the individual whose money he was responsible for investing:

"I am not in the business of predicting general stock market or business fluctuations. If you think I can do this, or think it is essential to an investment program, you should not be in the partnership."

And he was not exaggerating about that point. He *never* predicted stock movements for others; he predicted them for himself and for himself only.

At the same time he could always remind his investors that he had his own money placed in each partnership as well as the investor's money. The way he put it was pure Buffettese:

"So we are all eating our own cooking."

He constantly reminded his investors that he could make mistakes as well as anyone else could. But he usually had a safety net out there to get him past the bad spots. He always bent over backwards to be fair and honest with his partners, even if he did spin out some of his remarks with a twinkle in his eye. Note the dry wit when he wrote in 1962:

"I believe in establishing yardsticks prior to the act; retrospectively, almost anything can be made to look good in relation to something or other."

Buffett wanted his partnership to be something different from the type of fund then prevalent on Wall Street. He thought of *that* as committee-think, in Orwellian terms. His was different—different, if unorthodox, for a very good reason.

"My perhaps jaundiced view is that it is close to impossible for outstanding investment management to come from a group of any size," he wrote in 1965.

An episode in late 1963 showed the benefits of Warren Buffett's individualistic approach. American Express became involved in what came to be known as the "salad oil scandal." It almost ruined the company. In the crisis, Warren Buffett read the situation in his own special way—and reacted to it according to his own lights.

Briefly, an American Express subsidiary mistakenly certified the existence of a huge amount of salad oil stored in a certain warehouse. Suddenly an alert employee discovered that the salad oil did not exist—and that the subsidiary was liable for hundreds of millions of dollars' worth of claims in the nonexistent oil.

On news of this discrepancy, American Express's stock dropped from 60 to 56½ on November 22, 1963. President Kennedy was assassinated the very same day, and the stock market closed. On Monday, the stock was down to 49½.

The perpetrator of the salad oil scam was a white-collar crook recognized as such, Anthony De Angelis. He had invented the huge holding of salad oil in the American Express warehouse, had then borrowed money on the vegetable oil, had bet the money on vegetable oil futures, and had unfortunately lost.

He was arrested. Of course the money was gone. American Express would have to pay its creditors for De Angelis's scam. And the company was in bad trouble, even though it had millions of dollars in its traveler's check business. It was the credit card business that was going to suffer the most if people lost faith in the company.

Warren Buffett went to his favorite restaurant in Omaha, Ross's Steak House. He spent some time in a rather unusual fashion, chatting with the clerk at the cash register. He was watching the patrons as they brought out their credit cards to pay their checks. As far as he could tell, there was no decline in the number of American Express cards used.

Buffett checked out several other companies and determined that the credit card business of American Express was still on a solid footing—at least in people's minds. And on that information, he invested 40 percent of the Buffett Partnership—roughly $13 million—in American Express stock that was then going at $35 a share, way down from its high of $62.

To quote Warren Buffett: "A great investment opportunity occurs when a marvelous business encounters a one-time huge, but solvable, problem."

Warren Buffett violated one of his own most important rules in the American Express deal: never pay more than 25 percent of the partnership money in one investment.

But look what happened. American Express stock tripled in the next two years. Later Buffett told the *Omaha World-Herald* that he had held the stock for four years, selling out at a good profit.

He had never thought it good investment policy to do the same thing in the stock market as everybody else was doing. When he invested a sum, he selfishly put it where he thought it would do him the most good. By the same token, he did not feel it was always necessary *not* to do what everyone else was doing. Either way could lead to self-destruction.

The beginning of 1965 saw the Buffett Partnership with assets of $17,454,900. Buffett and his wife were carrying just over $2,000,000 of that. By the end of the year, the partnership's net assets had reached $26 million—all from the $105,000 that had been invested ten years earlier. His letter to his partners on January 10, 1966, included a little joke about the amount of money he and his wife were making, part of their private "war on poverty."

It was in 1965 that Warren Buffett's letters to his partners began to exhibit just a bit of crotchetiness. What caused his unease was the fact that the stock market seemed to be overheating just a bit—at least in his eyes. He wrote that he felt the old adage of "Bigger is better" did not work all the time anymore since there was no real long-term advantage in *overvaluing* stocks.

Yet in 1965 the Buffett Partnership showed what a phenomenal record he had set by his judicious manner of investment. Every single year from 1962 through 1966 Buffett had beaten the Dow by at least 10 percent. For example, in 1962 the Partnership had advanced 13.9 percent. The Dow had retreated 7.6 percent. In 1963 the Dow rose only 20.6 percent—"only" in relation to what Buffett's stock had done in gaining 38.7 percent. In 1964, the Partnership went up 27.8 percent; the Dow went up 18.7. In 1965 the Partnership zoomed up an unbelievable 47.2

percent, with the Dow rising 14.2 percent. And in 1966 the partnership rose 20.4 percent, with the Dow going down 15.6 percent.

Over the ten years of its existence, the Buffett Partnership had made 1,156 percent over its initial investment. The Dow had done well, too, rising 122.9 percent, but as Buffett modestly pointed out in a letter in 1967, the Partnership in 1966 marked an all-time high in its performance record compared to the Dow average—a total advantage of 36 points!

Nonetheless, Buffett was still fretting about the overheated market, which simply showed no signs of cooling off. In the letter, he railed against giving in to the forces at work on the market and selling, since overvaluing went against his basic instincts.

He was pessimistic in October 1967, apprehensive about market conditions that he did not like the looks of, and he warned of specific conditions—especially overheating in the market—that would make it harder for investors to work in the future.

By the time 1968 rolled around, however, he was a bit more upbeat. And he did not call up the old bugaboo of the overheated market at all. He would write that 1967 was, in the words made famous by Frank Sinatra, "a very good year" for him. The Partnership made solid gains of $19,384,250. Buffett earned a taxable income of $27,376,667—his stake in what he called "The Great Society of April 15"—that is, high tax revenues for the feds.

By July 1968, however, he had changed his tune just a bit. The old worry about the market crept back into his July 11, 1968, letter to investors in the Partnership, and he also pointed out he was no prophet, particularly in the stock market. But short-term profits seemed to be taking the edge off long-term benefits. Moreover, he was uneasy about the immense amounts of money being made by speculators. The suspicion existed in his mind that the whole thing could come tumbling down at any minute and throw the financial world into a turmoil.

By January 1969 Warren Buffett was reporting that the Partnership had risen an absolutely unbelievable 58.8 percent for the year. The Dow rose 7.7 percent during the same time period. This made Warren Buffett even more nervous about the market. For a hot market can pick the pockets even of the astute, he pointed out.

In May 1969 he was reporting that the investing environment was getting more and more negative and frustrating. And the only way to slow down the race for money, Buffett concluded, was to pull out.

And pull out he did.

He stopped playing the game at the end of 1969, liquidating the Buffett Partnership and giving the partners options to invest again or take the money and run.

He sent a letter of apology to the partners on February 15, 1970, explaining why he had made the hard decision to get out of the market temporarily with the Partnership, and trying to give them good reasons for the move he had made.

He pointed out that he was not in sync with current market conditions. He was particularly adamant about not investing where he felt it unwise to invest, even though the profits from doing so might increase his worth substantially.

He did not want to make quick profits so that he would look good. He wanted solid holdings that would make more for him in the long run. And since he couldn't invest in the market in its present overheated condition, he was closing down the Partnership to wait for better times.

Warren Buffett's reading of the stock market in that letter to his partners was right on target. Although he would not be proved right for three years or so, he had accurately predicted what was going to happen.

It was the stock market's disastrous downturn in 1973–74 that caused many people to suffer "permanent loss of capital," just as he had warned. Buffett, of course, was not one of them; he had read the picture right. He had also saved the money of those who had invested in the investment partnership he had founded.

CHAPTER SIX

Berkshire Hathaway

Warren Buffett was never a man to put *all* his eggs in one basket and ignore other possibilities in the investment field. In fact, while he was working the Buffett Partnership to the hilt, he was also studying every other stock he could find that might be of interest to him. By the time he closed down the Buffett Partnership in 1969, he had already opened up a brand-new field of endeavor: the purchase not only of stock, but of a company as well.

The name of the company was Berkshire Hathaway.

Berkshire Hathaway itself was a combination of the Berkshire Cotton Manufacturing Company, based in Providence, Rhode Island, and the Hathaway Manufacturing Company of New Bedford. Both were textile manufacturing companies that had been joined to create a textile giant in New England, for many years the traditional place for the manufacture of cotton and synthetic textiles.

Berkshire Cotton Manufacturing Company, incorporated in 1889, was a textile behemoth that once produced one-quarter of all the fine cotton made in the United Sates. It had been created by a man named Samuel Slater, who had built the first U.S. cotton mill in Pawtucket, Rhode Island, in 1793.

Slater's firm was a forerunner of Berkshire. In fact, one of Slater's carpenters, Oliver Chace, built his own mill in Rhode Island in 1806. With the rich harvest of cotton from the South, the mills began to turn out cloth for clothing and fabrics.

Chace was the activator. A century and a half later, his descendants controlled the Berkshire operation, which was composed of a dozen-odd textile plants spinning out fabrics for all purposes. World War II, with its demand for fabrics for uniforms, pushed Berkshire and its mills into a profitable wartime venture. Malcolm Chace, the president of Berkshire, seemed to have struck a gold mine—while the war lasted.

Actually, the days of King Cotton were over, at least in New England. World War II had given the ailing industry a false sense of security. The simple operation of turning out cotton fabrics was not enough to sustain an industry; the number of textile mills began diminishing immediately after the war.

Chace had a feeling that perhaps the days of his company were numbered.

Meanwhile Hathaway Manufacturing Company, founded in 1888 by Horatio Hathaway, had followed a similar pattern. While business was slow at the turn of the century, World War II had given the industry such a shot in the arm that Hathaway also prospered.

With the war ended, a lot of the smaller competitors of Berkshire and Hathaway got into other lines of business, or followed the fleeing workers to the South, where there were better prospects for making money—and for keeping jobs in the cotton business.

Hathaway was run by Seabury Stanton, an old New Englander whose grandfather had been a whaler. He saw the industry for what it was: a lame and dying duck. But he decided to do something about it. His intention was to modernize the operation and branch out into new fashions, into curtains, and into things like suit linings and so on. To do this formidable job, he invested $10 million of his family's fortune in the business. As a result, Hathaway was one of the first of the New England mills to exploit the development of rayon. But Hathaway's biggest advantage lay in its suit linings.

Then in 1954 a hurricane hit, and it flooded the plant. The best course of action would have been finally to leave New England for the South, where all the many other mills were now located. But Stanton was stubborn.

He knew Berkshire was in straits as dire as his. That led him to the idea of a merger. In 1955 the two companies did merge. Berkshire Hathaway, Inc., was an immediate giant. It ran fourteen separate textile plants. It hired twelve thousand workers. Its yearly sales were $112 million. The headquarters moved to New Bedford, Massachusetts. Stanton became president. Chace became CEO. Berkshire Hathaway was at that time the only surviving textile manufacturer of any appreciable size in the entire New England area.

Stanton had a clear vision of what he wanted Berkshire Hathaway to be and he continued to pour his family money into it. He scrapped the ancient equipment in many of the mills, bought new machinery, installed it, and sped up production. The ancient looms were modernized. The product was good, as were the prospects.

Stanton wanted production. Unfortunately, he had no concept of the bottom line at all. That is, he knew zilch about the difficult marketing problem that textiles were facing at that time. The Southern plants were running Berkshire Hathaway ragged; they manufactured and sold at a much lower price than the New England mills. Berkshire Hathaway was dying, even with all the money Stanton was pumping into the plants. It wasn't the product at all; the bottom line said that it was the *marketing* of the product!

Seabury Stanton lorded it over his employees as president of the company. He also lorded it over his brother, Otis Stanton. Yet Otis was an essential piece in the interlocking mechanism of Berkshire Hathaway. Otis was the man who sold the material to its buyers. Unlike Seabury, he was warm and friendly—and persuasive. He was constantly at war with Seabury, who thought production of the material was the virtual end of the textile industry, and to hell with salesmanship!

Competition from the South was killing the company, and Seabury couldn't see it. He ignored all the obvious signals as to where Berkshire Hathaway was headed. The 1960s were the years that foretold the end of the business. Berkshire Hathaway was down to seven plants. Stanton had poured $11 million back into the business. It wasn't helping a bit.

The plant's modernization was completed in 1962. And that year, ironically—and tragically—Berkshire Hathaway lost $2.2 million.

There was bad blood in the family. The feud that had been simmering between Otis and Seabury finally boiled over. Seabury Stanton wanted to name his son, Jack Stanton, to succeed him as president. Otis was livid. He saw Jack as Seabury's alter ego—another aloof, cold-eyed stone face. Jack was acting as the company treasurer in 1962, the year the money really hemorrhaged.

When the two companies, Berkshire and Hathaway, had merged in 1955, the stock was selling at 14¾ a share. By 1963, the stock was down to 8⅛—45 percent off the original figure.

Enter Warren Buffett.

Warren knew all about Berkshire Hathaway's troubled situation. He had spotted the company as far back as the time he was working at Graham-Newman in the 1950s.

But he had been unable to persuade Howard Newman to buy, even though Newman had gone up to investigate the company and had been impressed.

Now, in 1962, with the stock below $8 a share, Warren Buffett's interest mounted once again. Berkshire had $16.50 a share of working capital; $8 a share was a steal. Buffett brought some of it for his Buffett Partnership. He bought more in 1963, and was, by that time, the biggest shareholder in the company.

But nobody outside his own associates knew it. He was using a broker to locate and purchase the stocks for him. But as always, word finally leaked out, and it was soon known that Warren Buffett was buying up Berkshire Hathaway stock.

What for?

With his identity no longer a secret, Buffett decided to give the textile plant the once-over in person. He called ahead and learned that Jack Stanton, the treasurer, had copies of Berkshire's reports from way back. Buffett told Stanton that he wanted to visit the plant. Stanton agreed. He would have Ken Chace act as his tour guide.

Ken Chace—no relation to Malcolm Chace, incidentally, in spite of the same peculiar spelling of the name— was an employee at Berkshire Hathaway whom Otis Stanton was already considering as a possible president to replace Seabury Stanton. But neither Seabury nor Jack knew Otis's mind on this little ploy.

Chace was a local boy who by dint of hard labor had worked his way up to vice president of manufacturing. But he knew the ins and outs of textile production. He answered all Warren Buffett's questions as best he could. Buffett wanted to know all about the marketing, the machinery. He wanted to know what Chace thought should be done, where he thought the company was going. He asked questions about the technical end of production, and what kind of goods they were selling, and to whom they were selling.

Chace told him the truth. He had no reason to cover anything up. Meanwhile, Buffett knew that he had met an honest man who might be of assistance to him later on.

Seabury Stanton was no fool. He found out all he could about Buffett and in major panic he realized that Berkshire Hathaway might be under attack for a takeover. Berkshire Hathaway immediately offered to buy shares back from Warren Buffett's Partnership. Buffett realized that Stanton had sensed the possibility of a buyout. He realized that he would make a great deal of money by selling the stock he had in hand to Stanton. As a matter of fact he agreed to the deal, but signed no papers on it. It was just something that might work out in the future.

Eventually Seabury Stanton and Warren Buffett met to work out the details of the sales of the stock back to Stanton. The story went that they were only three-eighths of a point apart on the price. Buffett was all ready to sign the contract and sell—but he was annoyed with Stanton. He felt the man hadn't been forthright with him. And he suddenly turned stubborn himself. Typical Buffett.

The deal fell through.

Meanwhile, Buffett's broker continued to locate and hold shares of Berkshire Hathaway for him.

Finally Warren Buffett met with Ken Chace at the Plaza Hotel in New York. The two of them went outside and strolled about on Central Park South and across to Central Park.

"I'd like to have you become president of Berkshire Hathaway," Warren told Chace. "How do you feel about that?"

A stunned Ken Chace did what he had to do with this offer he couldn't refuse: he agreed wholeheartedly.

Buffett told Chace he had enough votes now to exert control over the company and to have Chace elected president. He even was able to get Otis Stanton to agree to sell, if Buffett offered to buy out Seabury Stanton. Otis and Seabury were always on opposite sides of *anything*.

Meanwhile, Jack Stanton wanted to fight off the buy-out, but his father didn't want to get into a messy proxy battle. He vetoed the suggestion. That was the end of the fight.

Before the board meeting on May 10, 1965, Buffett was secretly appointed a director of the company. Seabury Stanton opened the meeting, read through the agenda, then resigned. So did Jack Stanton. They left the board-room. Things went smoothly from that instant on. Ken Chace was voted president. Warren Buffett became chair-man of the executive committee. Otis Stanton became a member of the board. Malcolm Chace retained the title of board chairman. But in essence, Warren Buffett was in charge of Berkshire Hathaway.

The stock closed at $18.

Warren Buffett handed down his orders to Ken Chace after the meeting was over. He had no demands at all to voice. He didn't even tell Chace how much profit he wanted him to bring in. He did want, of course, a good profit. And he wanted a lean operation. He thought Chace would be able to manage that for him. What *counted*, of course, was the profit as a percentage of the capital in-vested. He had high hopes of being pleased with what would happen.

"I'd rather have a $10 million business making 15 per-cent than a $100 million business making 5 percent," Buf-fett told Chace. "I have other places I can put the money."

In 1966 and 1967, the textile business was making money hand over fist. The money simply rolled in. Meanwhile, Ken Chace was following Buffett's instruc-tions. He was doing all the cutting back he could man-age. Inventories were reduced to the lowest possible levels. The fixed assets were trimmed. The company seemed to be making a great deal of profit because of its lean-and-mean condition.

To the people who held shares of Berkshire Hathaway stock, there was little indication that the hand of Warren Buffett was controlling the company's actions. The annual reports came from Ken Chace and Malcolm Chace. But behind the scenes things were going on that nobody seemed to know about—or if they did, they said nothing.

Buffett was still buying all the Berkshire Hathaway stock he could lay his hands on. By January 1967, Buffett Partnership owned 59.5 percent of Berkshire Hathaway, and by April 1, 1968, it owned almost 70 percent of Berkshire. His total stake in Berkshire Hathaway was acquired for about $14 million, according to a story in *Forbes* magazine dated October 21, 1991.

Then suddenly things began to happen that were to become important to the stockholders of Berkshire Hathaway. Buffett had been looking around for some valuable underpriced holdings to buy into. And he found one in an Omaha insurance firm.

National Indemnity Company was owned by Jack Ringwalt, a man who knew who Warren Buffett was and who was keeping his eyes on Buffett's actions in the stock market. Ringwalt's insurance company had started back during the Depression, when he provided insurance specifically for taxicabs. His success at providing insurance for cabbies, who would probably be the last people any insurance company would want to indemnify, gave him further ideas about selling insurance to people who were unlikely to be good prospects for it.

Nosing about among his associates and acquaintances, Buffett had discovered from an Omaha broker friend what kind of price Ringwalt had put on his company. And so the next step was inviting him in for a talk at Kiewit Plaza.

The dialogue with Ringwalt bounced back and forth

as that of two cronies might, but in the end Warren got just what he wanted. He found out that Ringwalt had no hard-and-fast reason for *not* selling his company to someone who might offer good money for it. In fact, Ringwalt told Buffett frankly that he thought nobody in his right mind would want to buy it.

After some more sparring, Buffett asked him what he thought the stock was worth. Ringwalt said that the stock was selling at $33 a share, but that he knew it was worth more than that. He put its true value at about $50 a share.

Buffett nodded. He thought it was a fair price. And he offered to buy out Ringwalt. The two struck a deal, with Warren paying $8.6 million for the company.

Now there was one difference this time in Warren Buffett's negotiations. He was purchasing the stock not for Buffett Partnership, but actually for Berkshire Hathaway, the company for which he was acting as chairman of the executive committee.

What Warren Buffett was after in purchasing stock in National Indemnity Company was the simple matter of capital. He needed money to invest in other companies. And the really lovely thing about an insurance company was the fact that the capital was always up front, on tap, ready for use.

The money generated by National Indemnity Company for Berkshire Hathaway was put to almost instant use. Buffett was still looking around for underpriced companies. He was constantly adding to his list. His next target was the Illinois National Bank & Trust Company. He bought 97 percent of it early in 1969 for Berkshire Hathaway. The company was located in Rockford, Illinois, and had been run since 1931 by a hardworking, serious businessman named Eugene Abegg.

Abegg came up the hard way, working his way meticulously through the morass of the Depression. When the bank was practically on its last legs, he was able to scrape up the money to purchase the low-rated establishment and get it going again. This was a bank fashioned in the dream formula so loved by Warren Buffett.

At the time Abegg rescued the bank, almost all the banks in the same area were broke. The Illinois National Bank & Trust was, too. But Abegg pitched in, worked hard in a community that was trying desperately to recover from the ravages of the Great Depression, and constructed a $100 million base of deposits to keep it from going insolvent. His main claim to fame in Buffett's eyes was the fact that he had produced an earnings-to-assets ratio that was the highest among commercial banks. That meant something to Buffett.

Abegg was seventy-one years old when he sold out to Warren Buffett, and yet he continued to run the bank—because Buffett wanted him to stay. In a way, Abegg was similar to Ken Chace, of Berkshire Hathaway, who kept working for the company even after Buffett had purchased it. As a matter of fact, Abegg worked for Buffett through the bank until he was eighty years of age.

The secret of Warren Buffett's effect on these people who came into contact with him was that he was strictly a money-handling man. He was not a person who wanted to get hands-on thrills out of running a bank, or an insurance company, or whatever. For that matter, Jack Ringwalt at National Indemnity had stayed on the job after Buffett bought him out, just like Chace and Abegg. Buffett quite honestly told all these men exactly what he intended to do—look after the money.

And he stuck to his promise in all cases. They all stayed with him until they themselves determined it was time to retire. Buffett had that effect on businesspeople because of his character and his actions in running businesses and tending to the money.

Warren Buffett was also reading the writing on the wall. He knew New England textiles were on the way out. He wanted to get money away from textiles and into things like insurance, banking, and publishing.

It was during this time that Buffett bought the Newspapers of Omaha, Inc., a group of weekly papers in Omaha. He also bought Blacker Printer, Inc., another outfit in the publishing business.

Buffett was siphoning the money in Berkshire Hathaway out of the textile industry and getting it into something that was more viable. That was his plan. And finally in 1968 he closed the smaller of Berkshire Hathaway's mills in Rhode Island. And a year later, in 1969, he shut down entirely the business started way back when by Horatio Hathaway.

Berkshire Hathaway was safe from any drainage by its own plants at the time Buffett dissolved Buffett Partnership. In 1970, Warren Buffett became the owner of 29 percent of Berkshire Hathaway's stock. He took the liberty of installing himself as its chairman. He then sat down and began composing a letter to shareholders in Berkshire Hathaway's annual report as he had done with his stockholders in Buffett's Partnership.

To show how Buffett's actions had worked, in 1970, Berkshire's textile profits were a measly $45,000. But it brought in $2.1 million from insurance and $2.6 million from banking.

CHAPTER SEVEN

GEICO, Sun Newspapers, *Washington Post*

Now that Warren Buffett had devised the proper vehicle for his upcoming investments—that is, the purchase of the company that had been Berkshire Hathaway—he could concentrate more on the two types of stock that had always interested him the most.

Publishing.

And insurance.

His interest in publishing had been generated in his early years by the work he did in delivering newspapers—especially the *Washington Post.* It was the thing that made his life in Washington bearable during those particularly bleak growing-up years. And as one might expect, he had always been an avid reader of all kinds of publications.

But—insurance?

Insurance is a business with a peculiar difference to it, one that made it important to Warren Buffett. Most companies are started with what must be called venture capital—that is, a stash of money has to be on hand in order to get the fledgling corporation started up. Not an insurance company. The reason is obvious: The income in the form of policy payments comes first, then the pay-off, or payout. That is, the money is all up front and in the company's coffers before a dollar is paid out in claims of any kind. This pool of money has always been known as the "float."

What an investor like Buffett needed was the float—the working capital to purchase good stocks and good companies without going into deep debt or borrowing money to make the purchases.

And once the Berkshire Hathaway deal was consummated and he owned the company, Buffett wanted money to buy into more and more stocks. National Indemnity, within its healthy float, fit the bill, as did the Government Employees Insurance Company in Fort Worth, Texas.

GEICO had caught Buffett's attention years before when he had been working for his mentor at Graham-Newman. Now Warren was watching it attentively: the company was in trouble and needed help, the kind that Warren Buffett could give it. At a price, of course. GEICO insured certain selected automobile drivers who tended to have fewer accidents than the average—that is, professional drivers who had to drive vehicles in their work for the government.

It was the brainchild of Leo Goodwin, an accountant who sold insurance in San Antonio, Texas. From his piles of research on drivers of vehicles of all kinds, Goodwin came up with the fact that employees who worked for the government—at federal, state, and local levels—had fewer accidents than any other type of worker. To Goodwin this looked like a good pool of insurees; if the statistics proved out, the money would be coming in, and very little would be going out.

He knew, from his accounting work and his insurance selling, that the biggest cost to an insurance company was in marketing the product—that is, in advertising and selling the insurance policies in the first place. For government workers, there was no need for expensive advertising campaigns: government employees were a captive species. Insuring them directly would cut out the insurance agent, the middleman in the game, and stream-line the whole operation.

There was another captive market as well as govern-ment workers, Goodwin realized. Military personnel drove their own cars as much as government workers, and they too were easily insured directly without the aid of an agent. And so the target market was composed of government and military drivers.

Goodwin had a great idea, but he did not have great funds with which to make it come alive. He searched out someone to bankroll the deal, and found one eventually in a Fort Worth banker named Cleaves Rhea. In the end, Rhea invested $75,000 in the new company, with Good-win anteing up $25,000. Goodwin got 25 percent of the stock; Rhea, 75 percent.

It was no walk in the park. Goodwin and his wife, Lillian, worked a long day almost every day of the year, spending their weekends untangling customers' com-plaints and trying to straighten out other problems.

In the end Goodwin discovered that there were many more government drivers than military drivers—that was before World War II broke out—and in 1937, two years after GEICO was founded, the company moved directly to the seat of U.S. government, Washington, D.C., and rechartered on November 30.

The company prospered with the target group of gov-ernment drivers all around it. By 1940 it was beginning to make money—the first year of thirty-five years of con-tinual gain.

The Rhea family sold its 75 percent of the stock in 1948 to Warren Buffett's old company, the Graham-Newman Corporation. The company had a value then of about $2 million. The stock was split into 175,000 shares, trading at $20 a share.

The following year GEICO had netted $1 million and was expanding. Eventually, in 1952, it began insuring all state, county, and municipal employees. Premiums increased by more than 50 percent, to $15.2 million.

In 1958 Goodwin retired, with his company now worth $36.2 million. From two people in 1935, the company had grown to 985 employees writing 485,443 policies nationwide. The investors had done very well. A person with 100 shares of stock purchased in 1948—at a cost of $2,000—would have seen his stock rise in value to $95,000 on Goodwin's retirement date.

But the story did not end on that happy note. The insurance business was changing in the sixties and seventies, with no-fault coming into the picture, and inflation putting a crimp in all kinds of investment policies. The public itself was fed up with fat-cat insurance companies skyrocketing the rates into the stratosphere. Many states were mandating draconian regulations and reducing rates without thought of the insurers' fates.

By 1975 GEICO found itself on the brink of bankruptcy. Just like Berkshire Hathaway, the company needed a savior.

Enter Warren Buffett.

In May 1976 the board of directors of GEICO elected John Byrne chairman, president, and chief executive officer. Byrne appeared to have the qualifications to achieve a turnaround. It all depended on him.

What Byrne needed more than anything else was an infusion of quick money. But before the capital came in, he needed to solve two problems: the problem of rate increases and the problem of reinsurance.

To solve the problem of rate increases, Byrne initiated rigid cost controls and then set out to rewrite the book of the underwriting business.

Reinsurance is the assumption of part or all of the liability of one insurance company by another. Byrne was able to convince a number of GEICO competitors that GEICO should provide reinsurance relief for them.

As for the money, Byrne called upon Warren Buffett to help out. In a way, it was a desperation measure. But Byrne had heard of Buffett, and he knew that Buffett had had an interest in GEICO from a long way back.

In 1976, Buffett studied GEICO's situation once again. His interpretation was that the company still had good competitive advantages and could make a go of it in the long run. It was the short run that had buffaloed all attempts at a turnaround.

He met Byrne, and liked him. And, measuring the man in his usual quiet and laid-back fashion, he decided that Byrne would fill the bill perfectly. Buffett started the ball rolling by buying 1,294,308 shares of GEICO at $3.18. In the following five years, as GEICO began struggling out of its impasse, he followed that with $45.7 million in shares in the company.

By December 1980, Warren had 7,200,000 shares of GEICO stock. In effect, he owned one-third of the company at $1.31 per share, with a 5-for-1 split in 1992.

Warren Buffett analyzed his moves with GEICO later in these words:

"It [GEICO] wasn't necessarily bankrupt but it was heading there. It was 1976. It had a great business franchise which had not been destroyed by a lot of errors that had been made in terms of exploiting that franchise. And it had a manager."

From the beginning, Buffett was convinced that he could depend on a great deal of hard work, cooperation, and honesty from Byrne. And, in the book of Warren Buffett, those were important things—much more important than the movements of the stock.

"I felt he had the ability to get through an extraordi-

narily tough period there and to reestablish the value of
that franchise. They still were a low-cost operator. They
made all kinds of mistakes. They still didn't know their
costs because they didn't know what their loss reserves
should be and they got captivated by growth: they did
all kinds of things wrong but they still had the franchise."

The situation reminded Warren Buffett of an earlier
one he'd dealt with.

"It was similar to American Express in late 1963 when
the salad oil scandal hit it. It did not hurt the franchise
of the traveler's check or the credit card. It could have
ruined the balance sheet of American Express, but the
answer of course was that American Express with no net
worth was worth a tremendous amount of money."

That was where the two situations were parallel. Buffett tried to explain exactly how he had reasoned through
the debacle.

"And GEICO with no net worth was worth a tremendous amount of money, too, except it might get closed
up the next day because it had no net worth; but I was
satisfied that the net worth would be there. The truth is,
a lot of insurance companies for the ownership of it
would have put up the net worth. We would have put it
up. But they were trying to save it for the shareholders,
which is what they should have done."

In the long haul, it was the company itself, and the
business it had staked out for itself, that mattered—not
the ups and downs it might be going through at the
moment.

"It had a very valuable franchise. Take away all the
net worth. Let's just say that if GEICO paid out a $500
million dividend right now which would eliminate the
net worth of GEICO, would it still have a lot of value?
Of course it would have a lot of value. You'd have to do
something, you'd have to be part of another entity that

kept insurance regulators happy, but the franchise value is the big value in something like that."

With the help of John Gutfreund of Salomon Brothers, who underwrote a $76 million offering of GEICO preferred stock, the company worked its way out of disaster. But it didn't look so good at first. The offering was made in August. By November, it appeared that Salomon would be stuck with the entire $76 million.

And then, in the way of the marketplace, things began to clear up. Actually, Warren Buffett helped by taking 25 percent of the offering, making Berkshire Hathaway invested to the extent of $23 million in GEICO.

Six months later GEICO rose to 8⅛—four times its original rate. Buffett doubled Berkshire's stake, making himself the controlling investor. And Buffett's interest in GEICO never flagged. Once a year he would perform a Q. and A. with GEICO's executives.

While the insurance business tended to get worse for other insurers, GEICO seemed to be able to stay on track all right—especially with its refurbished image following the 1976 mess. What GEICO learned from that affair was that the insurance business was not a bed of roses at any time.

As Warren Buffett put it in his 1988 Berkshire annual report:

"If you want to be loved, it's clearly better to sell high-priced cornflakes than low-priced auto insurance."

Apparently he meant too that he didn't really need to be loved—since he was spending a proper amount of time with the people at GEICO in the insurance business.

In spite of his uncanny ability to do gigantic sums in his head, along with mathematical tricks of one kind of another, Warren Buffett still valued the common word. He was always interested in the newspapers he had money tied up in, particularly the Sun Newspapers, the neighborhood weeklies published in Omaha. In fact, he had a flair for digging up stories in the same manner that he dug up little-known facts and figures on companies he was interested in investing money in.

As he told the story, in 1972 he stumbled on an Internal Revenue Service regulation that required charitable foundations to disclose their assets. It was apparently a new statute; he had never heard about it before. But by putting his mind to a number of details he was familiar with, he uncovered a story that was worth journalism's number one honor: the Pulitzer Prize. The story began way back in 1917.

In that year a Catholic priest named Edward J. Flanagan rented a disreputable rundown house to help shelter five boys he had taken under his wing. This was the beginning of Father Flanagan's Boys Town, which later inspired the smash-hit 1938 motion picture starring Spencer Tracy and costarring Mickey Rooney. The motion picture made a hero out of Father Flanagan, and polished up the image of the great work such do-gooders were doing for their communities. In fact, Boys Town under the aegis of Father Flanagan did indeed expand a great deal from that first little house to become a kind of financial powerhouse.

Yes, kids were helped every day, but Boys Town could have poured more of the money it was raising into things for the kids rather than concentrating it in a huge stock portfolio. At least those were the rumors that were rife in Omaha—Warren Buffett's hometown.

When he learned of the IRS regulation, Buffett immediately telephoned the tiny newspaper chain and got hold of one of the editors there.

"I told our editor to get a copy of the Boys Town filing. I'd heard a lot of rumors during my fund days about Boys Town's large stock holdings."

The filing eventually came in. It showed that the rumors Buffett had been hearing were simply the tip of the iceberg. The truth was that there was a vast cesspool of stock holdings.

"Even I was staggered when we found that the home, which was constantly pleading poverty and caring for less than seven hundred kids, had accumulated assets of more than $200 million."

And that was the story Buffett gave to the Sun papers.

In addition to supplying the weekly papers with the main lead, Buffett also worked on the story with the writers and editors put in charge of it. In the end it was a blockbuster of an exposé, covering eight newspaper pages in the *Sun*. Buffett himself suggested the use of a line from Luke 16 as a headline for the story: "Give an account of thy stewardship."

The story was published in the *Omaha Sun* in March 1972, and eventually won a Pulitzer prize for the *Sun*.

This whetted Buffett's appetite for journalism—and for publishing in general. He was always waiting for a choice property to present itself, and eventually a property more choice than the *Sun* and its companions did come along.

It was the *Washington Post*—the newspaper that he had delivered during his high school days in Washington. What focused his attention on the *Post* was exactly what he sought in most of his stock deals. It was undervalued; or at least it appeared so to him.

And the 1973–74 stock market slump accentuated the extremely low price of the paper's stock, dropping it to $9 a share. *That* really made his journalistic pulse begin racing.

Buffett had studied the figures. He knew that the revenues of the Washington Post Company and its subsidiaries were supposedly worth $200 million. The subsidiaries included the *Post*, *Newsweek* magazine, the Times-Herald

Company, four television stations, and a paper company that supplied its newsprint.

The *Post* was worth four times the $200 million cited. It was a rule of thumb that a good newspaper might sell for about two and a half times annual revenues. And—looking at the bottom line—that meant the Washington Post Company was worth four times $200 million.

And so Warren purchased $10.6 million of Washington Post Company stock, which was a 12 percent stake of the Class B stock, or about 10 percent of the total stock. In doing so, he made Berkshire Hathaway the largest shareholder outside the Graham family, the owners.

And yet, shortly after he had bought the stock, the price fell from $10 million in 1973 to $8 in late 1974 despite the paper's winning a Pulitzer prize—and a much-needed burnishing—for Woodward and Bernstein's coverage of the Watergate scandal. The stock did not move ahead until 1976, after surviving a brutal strike; but after that year, it forged ahead to make Buffett's $10 million about $350 million.

In his own colorful way, Buffett once explained why he liked his investment in the *Washington Post.* It had to do with medieval warfare—castles, and joustings, and moats.

"There are some businesses that have very large moats around them and they have crocodiles and sharks and piranhas swimming around in them. Those are the kind of businesses you want. You want some business that, going back to my day, Johnny Weissmuller in a suit of armor could not make it across the moat. There are businesses like that."

And then he came out with what he had been going to say in the beginning:

"The trick is to find the ones that haven't been identified by someone else. What you want is a disguised television station or newspaper."

Warren Buffett served on the *Post* board until 1986. That was the year Berkshire Hathaway invested $512 million to help Capital Cities Communications buy the ABC network. When that transaction was complete, Buffett took a seat on the board of the resulting media giant called Capital Cities/ABC. Later, when Cap Cities/ABC was purchased by Walt Disney Company, Buffett rejoined the board of directors of the *Post*.

CHAPTER EIGHT

The *Evening News*

Through his continued association with Katharine Graham in Washington, Buffett soon learned of another afternoon paper that was ailing and up for sale, the *Buffalo Evening News*. When it became evident that the *Post* and Kay Graham did not want to purchase the ailing *Evening News*, Buffett sent out his envoys to seek more information about the foundering paper. He wanted to know if there were enough positive considerations to neutralize the negative financial details that surrounded the paper and its failure to prosper.

One reason he discovered for the paper's troubles was that the *Evening News*, being the voice of unionism in a strongly blue-collar union city, was finding it tough economic going with the many excellent contracts the Newspaper Guild had managed to wring out of it through the years. The *Evening News* was in the top 10 percent of all the wage brackets represented by the Newspaper Guild in the United States.

An even more serious problem was competition from Buffalo's morning paper, the *Courier-Express*. The competition was formidable because of a quirk in the papers' publishing schedules. The *Buffalo Courier-Express* published every day of the week, including Sunday; the *Buffalo Evening News* did not publish on Sunday. The difference had to do with an ancient agreement apparently made between the two families that published the papers. But the bottom line—the amount of money lost through this arrangement—was a serious detriment to the *Evening News*.

In short, the *News* beat the *Courier* on weekdays by about 268,000 copies, compared to 123,000. But—and it was a big "but"—the Sunday *Courier* sold 270,000 copies each week. *That* was the wrinkle that kept the *Courier* in business.

And Warren Buffett had a pretty good idea about what he could do to solve *that* problem.

But first Buffett had to scout around for some loose change that he could package to buy the newspaper, if indeed he did decide to do so. He had most of the essential information about the paper in his head already. In the late sixties he had picked up a little nugget of a company called Blue Chip Stamps. Blue Chip Stamps was now a subsidiary of Berkshire Hathaway.

The company provided one special advantage for Warren Buffett at this point. The money, like the money for an insurance company, was always up front. It was, in effect, another money tree for Buffett to pick from.

Blue Chip Stamps had begun business in 1956 as a trading stamp company. It provided two types of service. First, trading stamps could be used by a business organization to attract customers. Second, they could be used internally by any business for motivational purposes, to goad its sales force into action.

The trading stamp business peaked in the early 1970s. At that time Blue chip was worth more than $124 million; then revenues began to deteriorate because many supermarkets decided to convert from stamps to discount marketing. Also, service stations, which were once great users of trading stamps, found themselves faced with an unbelievable gasoline shortage at the beginning of the Near East crisis. Why promote sales of something that was in short supply already?

Then, in 1982, the supermarket that was responsible for 51 percent of Blue Chip's revenues opted out of the trading-stamp business.

The problems that Blue Chip had, however, did not affect the cash it had already accumulated, and Warren Buffett knew the cash was still there to be used.

The scouting reports on the *Buffalo Evening News* all looked good to Buffett. Once again, he approached Kay Graham to make sure that the *Washington Post* did not want to get into a bidding battle for the Buffalo paper so soon after settling the monstrous strike that had hobbled the *Post* for so long. The signals were very clear. The *Post* wanted no part of the Buffalo paper.

Meanwhile, Vincent Manno, called a "newspaper broker" in the trade, was working on a number of other deals for the *Evening News* with big city newspapers, but he was finding the going very hard. Through the grapevine, Buffett learned that Manno had been forced to reduce his asking price of $40 million to $35 million.

Buffett had been using Charlie Munger as a close associate more and more now that Munger was involved directly with Berkshire Hathaway, and he and his accomplice met with Manno on a weekend in 1977. The Omaha partners were wined and dined by Manno at one of those exclusive country clubs that used to appear as background in any golden age Hollywood movie that was set in Connecticut.

Then they got down to business in Manno's comfortable study at the house. The first offer from Buffett was $30 million. Manno shook his head. Too low. Actually, the offer was exceptionally high considering the newspaper's sickly profit for 1976.

Warren and Munger had gone over the numbers very carefully. The *News* had earned $1.7 million in 1976. But there were other considerations. The paper was languishing from inaction; it had no other serious ailments. Buffett felt that it could be made to produce a great deal more revenue. After all, the *Evening News* did outsell the *Courier-Express* by two to one during the week.

Warren and Munger went into a huddle. Munger wrote "$32.5" on a sheet of paper. It was handed to Manno.

The broker nodded. It was that simple. The papers were drawn up and signed and Warren Buffett was now the legitimate publisher of a big-city newspaper, an up-and-coming Hearst. And it had been done with Blue Chip Stamps money—every cent of the purchase price!

The *Evening News* had a very impressive printing plant, a massive structure that Buffett laughingly referred to as "Taj Mahal East" whenever he spoke of it. He and Munger had toured the plant during the weekend spent getting the contracts in order for the closing. Munger's pessimism had escalated appreciably as he stared at the palatial surroundings. He liked business things lean and hungry.

So did Warren Buffett. Yet this move was a very important new direction for him to be taking. And he liked what he had bought. His other "acquisitions" were simply corporations in which he owned a majority of stock. He not only owned this company lock, stock, and barrel, but he could do anything he wanted to *with* the *Evening News*.

Once the paperwork was out of the way, Buffett took over. And he began acting like a kid with a new toy. He had one big plan. And he let that one leak out at a party thrown for Munger and him by Murray Light, the editor of the paper. As they stood around in Light's backyard, Warren Buffett remarked offhandedly: "News happens twenty-four hours a day, seven days a week."

And that was telling it like it was. That was the big change he was going to make. He was going to come out with a new Sunday edition for the *Evening News*.

True to his backyard promise, Buffett instructed his editor to design a Sunday paper. And, in contrast to his usual hands-off approach in dealing with the companies he had invested money in, he made frequent visits to the plant, where he and Light would go over detail after detail of the new edition.

He loved it.

"Kay," he wrote, "I'm having so much fun with this it is sinful."

The new Sunday edition was promoted like mad by the *Evening News*. It would be started in November 1977. An intensive campaign was mounted to secure ads.

The *Courier-Express* wasn't about to stand still at this intrusion on its "private" preserve. It immediately sued the *News*, asking the courts to issue an injunction against their rival's new Sunday paper. The suit claimed that the *Evening News* was engaging in monopolistic behavior, publishing a money-losing paper on Sunday to kill the *Courier-Express* as a competitor and thus to establish a monopoly of one paper in Buffalo.

Although the *Evening News* intended to sell its Sunday edition for only thirty cents, against the *Courier-Express*'s fifty cents, Buffett argued that the *Evening News* was intended to earn a profit on Sunday rather than publish a kamikaze loss-leader. He would, he said, establish competition where it had never existed before, rather than inhibit it.

This was a new thing for Warren Buffett: battling a rival—and especially in court. He was feeling the sharp sting of criticism for the first time in his life. He had always been able to vanish from the scene of any confrontation almost without anyone's noticing. But now the *Courier-Express* hired Frederick Furth, a hotshot San Francisco lawyer, to turn the city of Buffalo against Warren Buffett, the unfeeling carpetbagger, the "Big Brother from Omaha."

Buffett weathered the attacks on his character well enough. He filed an affidavit that showed his earlier interest in newspapers—that is, his paperboy days in Washington with the *Post*—and his *Omaha Sun*'s Pulitzer prize.

A hearing on the injunction to suppress the new Sunday edition of the *Evening News* was held on November 4, 1977. Although Buffett handled himself as well as could be expected, his command over such a large sum of money as he had made him suspect, at least in the eyes of the spectators—mostly *Courier-Express* employees and their families, who would be out of luck if indeed the *Courier-Express* did fold because of the *Evening News*'s Sunday edition.

Buffett said that he did not believe that the new Sunday edition of the *Evening News* would affect the *Courier-Express* at all. He felt that quite probably the *Evening News* would be behind the *Courier-Express* in circulation anyway. And he told why he thought so.

"Well, you assume that the *Courier* has been publishing for many, many years, all alone in the market—that people's habit patterns are very strong. I shave my face on the same side first every morning and put on the same shoe first and people are creatures of habit. And the product that they have been receiving every day for a great many years has an enormous advantage."

The hearing was covered by all the newspapers nearby. On November 9, four days before the scheduled publication of the first Sunday paper, Judge Charles L. Brieant Jr. issued his ruling, issuing an injunction against the *Evening News*. He said that he thought the *Courier-*

Express would be able to prove at a trial that the *Evening News* was employing unfair tactics against its competitor.

But his most damning words came in the following statement, when he pointed out that if the new Sunday edition was not stopped, the *Courier-Express* would probably go out of business:

"There are only two newspapers now. If the plan works as I find it is intended to work, there will be but one left."

The judge's ruling was published throughout the area, giving the *Evening News* its worst dousing of negative publicity in years. Unfortunately Warren Buffett was the dark presence in the drama, a kind of menacing offstage villain waiting to grab the money and run.

Not only that, but all staff members of the *Evening News* had been enjoined by the court not to make any negative remarks about the *Courier-Express*. However, no one put any rein on the *Courier-Express*'s remarks about the *Evening News*. Advertisers and readers of the two papers were affected by the judge's statements, and ended up supporting the *Courier-Express*.

The injunction went into effect with the judge's ruling. It actually permitted the Sunday edition to be printed. However, the language of the injunction prohibited the paper from promoting, marketing, and circulating the new edition to advertisers and to potential readers.

After five weeks of publication of the Sunday edition, the *Evening News* had only 147 inches of ads, compared to 579 for the *Courier-Express*. The *Evening News* was in deep trouble. At the time, about one-fifth of Warren Buffett's personal fortune was involved in the *Evening News*. He had made a misstep that could not easily be corrected.

Almost overnight in this battle of the newspapers there were no holds barred. The two rival papers were suddenly engaged in a bloody circulation war.

The *Courier-Express* had been getting along on a meager budget. Now management was galvanized into action. Suddenly the pressroom was automated. Then the equipment was upgraded. The editor bought more comics to bulk out the copy. A bigger magazine was developed. The paper had split pages, outlook sections, new graphics. In addition to that, management ordered that the payroll be augmented by at least 25 percent.

Buffalo became a battlefield on which the troops of both papers roamed at will, trying to dig up news that was not evident. It would be worth the career of a reporter on the *Evening News* to be beaten out by one on the *Courier-Express*. Warren Buffett would have no mercy on those who did not succeed under him.

In addition Buffett knew what made a paper superior to its rivals. Too many cheaply printed papers cared only about the bottom line—that is, the ad revenues. Circulation continued to play a minor part in newspaper profits. In some papers what was called the "news hole"—that is, live stories, columns, and reading material of all kinds—was less than half the pages of the full newspaper. Ads dominated, leaving little for the customer to read.

Warren Buffett was a friend of the news hole, a friend of the loyal reader. He kept the hole big and he kept it sparkling.

"We made a point of having more news than the other paper," he later said. "If they had eight pages of sports, we were going to have more. All the traditional ratios— I told 'em to hell with it."

The circulation war continued—and not always to the good of the *Evening News*. In 1978 the *Courier-Express* simply beat the hell out of the *Evening News* by 100,000 papers every Sunday.

There were other considerations, too. A recession hit Buffalo, and the people who were out of work began worrying about the people on the *Courier-Express*. Would they be next? If the money man—Warren Buffett—had

his way, the *Courier-Express* would be dead. So they
thought. So they said.

Buffett cooperated in all kinds of promotion. He
would appear to meet big advertisers and local retailers
of importance. He would take part in whatever the
paper proposed.

"We did everything," he said. "We had these special
circulation teams. All week they would tell me, 'We got
828 starts this week, 750 starts this week.' Then, on Friday
night, I would get the draw for Sunday and we'd be
down to 412 or something."

Buffett was not worried about the big battle. That was
being fought out in the trenches by both newspapers. And
he had no doubt that in the end the *Evening News* would
win the war.

What he needed was a troubleshooter—a guy who
could go down to the shop once a month or so and
straighten out things that had gotten bollixed up. And
Buffett knew just the man he needed: Stan Lipsey, a good
friend, and the publisher of the *Omaha Sun*.

Eventually Lipsey, who initially did not want to dab-
ble in Buffalo's newspaper war, bowed to Buffett's pleas
and began visiting the shop every so often as an "assistant
to the publisher." He did what he could to repair any
damage that he saw being done. But the problem mostly
was that the newspaper was operating under the rather
strained mercy of a federal judge who allowed the opposition to police the *News*'s activities, to have access to the
News's records, and to have discovery over the *News*.

It showed up on the bottom line. In 1978, the *Evening
News* lost $2.9 million. It was the biggest drain on Buffett's
fortune to date. And yet he was staying upbeat about the
situation. For reasons of his own, he sensed that something might change for the better. And in April 1979, it
did.

The U.S. Court of Appeals in New York reversed the

injunction and the contempt citation and gave Judge Brieant this rebuke:

"Taking first the issue of intent, we find simply no evidence that Mr. Buffett acquired the *News* with the idea of putting the *Courier* out of business as distinguished from providing vigorous competition, including the invasion of what had been the *Courier*'s exclusive Sunday market. . . . All that the record supports is a finding that Mr. Buffett intended to do as well as he could with the *News* and was not lying awake thinking what the effect of his competition on the *Courier* would be. This is what the anti-trust laws aim to promote, not to discourage."

Shortly after the court's reversal, the Minneapolis Star & Tribune Company, owned by the Cowles family of Minneapolis, purchased the *Courier-Express*. Now the battle escalated a ratchet or two. The Cowleses had deep pockets, and the company did what it could for its Buffalo acquisition.

In 1979 Buffett took a real wallop in the wallet. The *Evening News* lost $4.6 million. This was the kind of loss neither Buffett nor Munger could take, since it drained money right out of their pockets and the pockets of the members of their investing families.

Buffett put the Sun chain—the weeklies published in Omaha—up for sale in 1980 and eventually got a taker. Lipsey moved to Buffalo to live there and work on the *Evening News*. In the war he had joined at the behest of Warren Buffett, Lipsey had become addicted to working on a big-city paper. And if not Buffett, *he* wanted to bury the *Courier-Express*.

Besides, Lipsey knew that Buffett really wanted him to be there to help out in a battle that was not an easy one, any way you looked at it.

The *Evening News* had always had problems with the unions it dealt with. Just before Warren Buffett had purchased the paper through the Blue Chip Stamps company, the thirteen unions had extended their benefits as far as they could, leaving the company in an almost-broke situation at the end of the year.

A notice appeared in the Blue Chip report in 1980:

"If any extended strike shuts down the *Buffalo Evening News*, it will probably be forced to cease operations and liquidate."

"Bluff!" muttered the unions.

"No bluff!" Warren Buffett shot back.

In late 1980, the delivery truck drivers posted their demands: they wanted new manning requirements, and pay for work even if it wasn't done. Warren Buffett said no. Ray Hill, of the Newspaper Guild, knew Warren Buffett was not bluffing. He advised the teamsters not to play their usual game of strike-while-the-iron-is-hot.

Martin Brogan, head of the teamsters, felt that Buffett wouldn't risk a strike in the midst of his battle with the *Courier-Express.* The teamsters walked. The pressmen stopped and pulled the page plates and the paper shut down.

Buffett called a meeting and ordered the staff to go home. If the drivers didn't return for the next Sunday edition, he would close the paper for good.

It was the teamsters who blinked, not Buffett. Work did resume. The battle of the Sunday editions continued, but after five years, the *Evening News* still trailed, 195,000 to 265,000. The money losses continued. Since Buffett had taken his big fling in the newspaper business, he had personally lost $12 million through the paper.

And then, in September 1982, a miracle: the *Courier-Express* folded. It had been hurt by trouble at the parent company in Minneapolis.

The day the *Courier-Express* expired, the *Evening News* changed its name to the *Buffalo News*. It also started a morning edition. In six months, Sunday circulation topped 360,000. Ad rates went up, reflecting the paper's increased readership. The paper became a sudden gold mine. The *Buffalo News* earned $19 million in its first year without competition. In the late eighties, the *Buffalo News* would earn more than $40 million a year.

The victory of the *News* over the *Courier* was a victory only for the people who owned it. The workers did not do at all well. When someone suggested that the company should institute profit-sharing for people in the news-room, Warren Buffett simply shook his head because, in his view, no one in the newsroom or in the journalistic area of the paper had anything to do with the profits or losses of the publication. Buffett explained what he meant in a little more detail to his stockholders in 1984.

He had learned from experience that a newspaper in a dominant position would always make good money. It had little to do, he went on, with the quality of the jour-nalism or the fame of the paper. A dominant paper— whether it was a first-rate paper or a third-rate paper— would always make money for its owners, so long as its dominance continued.

CHAPTER NINE

Capital Cities/ABC

The year 1977 was a watershed year for Warren Buffett—in a personal sense that had nothing whatsoever to do with his investment business or his stock market choices. What happened happened so swiftly and so unexpectedly that even the unflappable Warren was shaken.

That year, while Warren was totally occupied in his journalistic joust with the *Courier-Express* in Buffalo, his wife, Susan, had been doing her usual thing: accompanying Warren on their annual two-week vacation to New York City, acting as his partner at parties in Omaha, running the family just as usual—although there was a lot less of it around than ever before. In fact, the nest was empty.

Daughter Susie was now married and living out in California. She had graduated from college at the University of California at Irvine and had gotten a job nearby, working for Century 21. And she had also found herself a husband in the same area.

Howie, the elder son, had enrolled at Augustana College in Sioux Falls, South Dakota. But after a few semesters he had become bored with studying and had dropped out. He had inherited his father's business sense and was involved in starting up his own business, Buffett Excavating, near Omaha.

Peter, the youngest of the brood, was attending Stanford University.

And so there was little for Susan Buffett to do around the house except prepare a meal now and then for Warren and perform the obvious chores. Meanwhile, the outgoing Susan had become immersed in making public appearances as a singer: some years before she'd begun seriously to practice singing, and she had given concerts in various places in the Midwest.

Word went around. She was good. There was a professional polish to her work. People in show business with big names complimented her on her stage presence, and on her abilities in singing and acting.

It was an almost classic case of empty-nest syndrome. With the kids out of the house, and her husband deeply involved twenty-four hours of the day in his business enterprises, Susan Buffett had become aware that she needed to pay a little more attention to her own needs rather than subordinate herself totally to her husband's.

For months she continued her appearances as if they would go on forever that way, just little interruptions in her main job as wife to Warren Buffett. But in the back of her head she must have been reasoning it out.

In the fall of 1977, about the time Warren Buffett was fighting his hardest in Buffalo to win the circulation battle against the *Courier-Express*, Susan Buffett was moving toward a future where she could control more of her own destiny than she ever had before.

In September 1977 she simply packed up her bags and walked out. And it was no jaunt across the street or to the other side of town. She moved to San Francisco, rented an apartment, and settled down there for a while.

To the friends and associates of Warren Buffet this

was unbelievable. If anyone could have been considered the dedicated and lovable wife, it was Susan Buffett. But, like Warren, she was able to keep her true feelings well hidden and go on with her life in the usual way.

That is, up to the breaking point.

Even more shocked and depressed over this sudden move than Susan's many friends was her husband. He had a hard time trying to figure out what had happened. After all, the two of them had been getting along famously for years. What was the matter? He had made her a billionaire, too. That was the reason she was totally independent of him and could do what she liked, of course. But still . . .

He hadn't meant for her independence to enable her to fly away.

The children rallied around Warren as best they could—Susie flew in occasionally to spend some time at the house. Warren was, for a time, a broken man, mooning about and feeling sorry for himself—he, a man who never had a care in the world about personal things. The children soon accepted the situation, realizing that their mother did need her own life now that the household had been shrunken down to two people.

The break was in no way a desertion, or a final rupture. The two Buffetts talked to one another almost every day on the phone. And the vacation trips to New York continued, as did short stops in their Malibu home, and elsewhere.

It was a situation of parallel lives on separate planes rather than a break in toto. And eventually Warren began to recover somewhat. At first he had been unable to talk to other people, or see his friends, but soon he got over that and began to revisit all of his old haunts—playing bridge, poker, and so on.

It was actually Warren's wife who introduced him to Astrid Menks, a blond young woman who had a job as a waitress at an Omaha restaurant. Astrid was just one of the many friends that Susan had encouraged to call Warren, have dinner with him, see a movie with him, and the whole bag of tricks.

Astrid came to the house one night and fixed some soup for Warren. And the two began to hit it off. They were totally different people and it was a surprise to many of Warren's friends that they could become so cozy.

A Latvian who had escaped from persecution in the Old Country, Astrid had settled down in Omaha's artsy section—a seedy Greenwich Village–type setting—where artistes on the edge of society liked to spend their days and nights. And yet, here she was, doing quite well in catering to Warren Buffett's peculiar likes and dislikes—especially his unimaginative taste in cuisine.

Within a year of Susan's departure from the Buffett home, Astrid moved in and unpacked her things to become a fixture in the household. Soon it seemed that the household had always worked that way and that Warren had weathered whatever jolt he might have felt at the departure of his wife. And, in truth, Warren Buffett acted exactly the same then as he had for years before. He had always been aloof and detached from the details of life around him.

Nineteen seventy-seven was also the year Warren Buffett first became acquainted with and interested in a company called Capital Cities. He purchased 3 percent of the company for Berkshire Hathaway, but after a short time he sold the stock. Buffett admitted later on that he had been the victim of "temporary insanity" to do that. He should never have let it out of his grasp.

Capital Cities had started out as a small UHF radio station in Albany owned by the Hudson Valley Broadcasting Company. The "capital" city of the name was of course Albany.

Soon after graduating from Harvard Business School and serving a stint at Lever Brothers in New York City, a man named Thomas S. Murphy took a job at $18,000 a year as manager of Hudson Valley Broadcasting. This was a no-win situation. The station broadcast out of a home for retired nuns. Under Murphy's management, the company acquired another station and went public in 1957— at seventy-two cents a share.

Murphy teamed up with a man named Daniel Burke, the younger brother of James Burke, Murphy's classmate at Harvard, and began acquiring a number of broadcasting stations throughout the area. At this time the name of the company was changed to Capital Cities.

This operation, no matter how widespread it became with its acquisitions, was frugal. It was, in fact, the type of operation that set Warren Buffett's palms to itching. And that was the reason he dabbled in Capital Cities stock in 1977.

Buffett had developed great respect for Murphy in his dealings with him when he purchased the stock, and he particularly admired Murphy's straightforward way of coping with difficulties and his lack of phoniness and show. He thought of Murphy as a man of his own stripe. And Burke was similar in his straightforward ways.

Meanwhile, Leonard Goldenson, the man who had founded the ABC network in 1953, had decided that, at the age of seventy-nine, he was getting too old to run things at ABC; he was looking around for someone to buy the network. He had good people working for him, but they were not good managerial material at all. They were essentially network people—as they should be. No, what he wanted was some kind of good sensible caretaker, someone who could take the network off his own hands and operate it without losing it to some rival who might liquidate it into something not even resembling a network.

Goldenson had heard good things about Thomas Murphy and Daniel Burke. He studied the records of their dealings and kept his eyes on them until he felt he was able to make a decision about selling out to them. Finally he did: he was going to leave the company in their hands, if, of course, they wanted it. There was only one hitch. Murphy and Burke didn't have any money.

But Warren Buffett did. And that was the reason that quite suddenly one day in 1985 Buffett got a telephone call. It was Thomas Murphy, and his request stunned Buffett. Murphy told him that Capital Cities had just agreed to purchase the entire ABC network from Leonard Goldenson. The clincher was this:

"You've got to come and tell me how I'm going to pay for it!"

Buffett smiled. He had long had more than a passing interest in ABC. When International Telephone and Telegraph wanted to buy ABC in the late 1960s, the Justice Department had blocked the sale.

Buffett knew that the network was then in the hands of arbitrageurs. "Anyone could get control," he'd told an associate. "I sure wish I had the money." He had purchased a bit of ABC in 1979, and again in 1984. At the time of Murphy's frantic call to him, Warren Buffett already owned 2.5 percent of ABC's stock.

When Buffett answered Murphy's question, he had absolutely no intention of getting into the sale himself. What he did was give Murphy the advice he sought.

Buffett: "You better have a nine-hundred-pound gorilla. Somebody who owns a significant amount of shares who will not sell *regardless of price*."

Buffett meant someone who was loaded, someone who would be absolutely loyal to Murphy and to the company he had bought.

Murphy: "How about you being the gorilla, pal?"

But Buffett knew that it was not quite that easy. Sure,

he had the money. Money wasn't the problem. The problem was the Federal Communications Commission's "cross-ownership" rule. That rule forbade the company from owning both a TV station and a newspaper in the same town. Warren Buffett owned the *Buffalo News*, and ABC owned a TV station in Buffalo.

Sell the *Buffalo News*, Murphy suggested. That was the easy way out.

Buffett refused. "I promised the people there that I would never sell it. I told them, when they wrote my obituary it would say, 'He owns the *Buffalo News*.' "

Murphy got the point. He was straightforward and honest, too, and stuck to his word. Capital Cities would sell its TV station in Buffalo.

In that case, Buffett was in.

"We made the deal in about thirty seconds," Buffett reported.

Not quite true.

There was one other matter that would become a sticking point. It had to do with Buffett's position on the board of the *Washington Post* and also the board of Capital Cities as an owner. Warren did not want to give up his position at the *Post*. He asked Murphy for some time to consider his options. In the end he decided that if he kept his stock in the *Post* it would not hurt him to resign from the board.

In a later interview, Warren Buffett told a *New York Times* reporter: "I was up there on a Thursday morning on April 2, 1985. I said, 'How many shares do you want me to buy?' He said, 'What do you say?' I said, 'How's three million?' He said, 'Fine.' I said, 'What price should I pay?' He said, 'What do you think?' I said, '$172.50.' He said, 'Done.' " Eighteen percent of Cap Cities for half a billion dollars.

Cap Cities would then proceed to use the infusion of

equity from Berkshire Hathaway to finance its planned purchase of ABC.

But in the end that was not exactly the way it went. Talks bogged down between Joseph Flom, ABC's merger lawyer, and Bruce Wasserstein, First Boston's merger expert who represented the network, and Warren Buffett. The ABC men were agitating for more ABC shareholders.

In the end it was Warren and Wasserstein who worked it out. The agreement was that each ABC shareholder would get $118 in cash for each share, plus a warrant to buy one-tenth of a share of Capital Cities stock for two and a half years after the acquisition. Capital Cities would redeem the warrants at $3 for ninety days after the merger.

The real value of the warrants was that they gave ABC shareholders a right to buy some Capital Cities shares at $250. If the merger worked out, and the price rose above that, warrant holders would make a pile. And indeed they did.

In the end, Warren Buffett became a director of Capital Cities/ABC. And he agreed to vote with management for eleven years—so long as Tom Murphy or Daniel Burke was still in charge.

In the annual report he explained how he had helped Cap Cities get together enough money to pay the American Broadcasting Companies $3.5 billion to take over their ownership. Buffett explained that there would be little investing and shifting of money about, and said that some things just took time to happen—and he would be happy to wait in the wings for things to straighten out at ABC.

He sketched a dreamworld where those in charge of ABC would be able to concentrate wholly on ABC in order to make it a competitive network rather than be at the mercy of fast-talking and fast-fixing financial experts who were in the game to make a quick buck and then move on to another rapidly developing deal.

He had some fun with another point in the same annual report: he reviewed the past in which he had sold Berkshire's holdings in the ABC network for $43 per share in 1978–80 and was now paying $172.50 per share for the very same holdings. He asked for the indulgence of his readers and begged for just a little more time to come up with a "snappy answer" to satisfy any critics of this somewhat strange un-Buffetlike buy-high, sell-low strategy.

Capital Cities was an excellent investment, in spite of the back-breaking struggle to turn around the ABC network. In addition to the ABC network, Cap Cities owned seven ABC radio networks with 2,200 affiliates, radio's largest advertising medium; eight television stations; and twenty-one radio stations. It held 80 percent of the ESPN sports cable channel, which reached 60 percent of U.S. households, more than any other cable network. It published newspapers, trade journals, shopping guides, business publications, books, and records; provided research services; and distributed information from databases.

Cap Cities also owned 38 percent of the Arts & Entertainment Network, a cable programming service devoted to cultural and entertainment programming; one-third of Lifetime, a cable programming service devoted to women's lifestyle and health programming; and half of Tele-Munchen GmbH, a Munich–based television and theatrical production/distribution company with interests in cinemas, a Munich radio station, and a German cable television program service.

The ABC Television Network pulled itself together in spectacular fashion. For many years, it had the top-rated early morning program for TV viewers. Only recently was *Good Morning America* dethroned from its top spot by NBC's *Today*.

In news, ABC did generally very well. As head of the news department, Roone Arledge produced *World News*

Tonight. With Peter Jennings as anchor, *World News Tonight* was rated the number one early evening news program in 1989, the first time ABC took the top spot since it began broadcasting the evening news in 1953. In 1990 *World News Tonight* was the most-watched evening news broadcast.

In prime-time and late-night news broadcasting, *20/20* with Hugh Downs and Barbara Walters and *Nightline* with Ted Koppel were big successful shows.

In 1989 ABC News began broadcasting *Primetime Live,* with hosts Sam Donaldson and Diane Sawyer.

In sports, ABC was one of the great innovators. The network came up with *ABC Monday Night Football,* hosted at one time or another by Howard Cosell, Frank Gifford, and Dandy Don Meredith. In its heyday, it was the most popular prime-time program among men viewers.

As for sitcoms with the highest ratings, *Roseanne,* starring Roseanne Barr, was a top-rated show during the late eighties and early nineties until it was replaced by another ABC sitcom, *Home Improvement,* starring Tim Allen. Another big hit, *America's Funniest Home Videos,* also scored big for ABC.

Hard times hit in 1990 when earnings for the second quarter were way below expectations. The stock plunged from $588.50 to $533, down $55.50 from the previous day's close. Then it rose to $633, but fell almost 23 percent to $488. It was a yo-yo kind of world for a while.

The networks were all coming under attack from their new competitors—the cable channels, the new cable networks, and the direct access television networks. Warren Buffett told the Berkshire Hathaway annual meeting in 1987:

"The networks used to own people's eyeballs, and they don't anymore. The people at Cap Cities are sensational managers, but they may have to be."

In spite of the tough years, when the Super Bowl aired

on January 27, 1991, it cost a sponsor $800,000 for a thirty-second commercial that would reach 100 million Americans.

In a 1985 article in *Investment Decisions,* Warren Buffett explained his rationale for purchasing ABC with Murphy and Burke in position there. The idea behind the deal was to promote a kind of stability in the network that would ordinarily not be present, what with the widely diffused ownership of its voting stock. With Murphy and Burke in place, the temptation to shift money about could be kept to a minimum.

The very fact of one man's ownership of a very large amount of capital might make the average manager of a large corporation nervous and worried about a sudden shift of big sums. With Buffett holding the money, however, no one at ABC had to fear any sudden upheavals of that nature, knowing Buffett's track record of solid investment methodology.

Indeed, Buffett assured management that there would be no such game playing, no secret deals in the works, with everything straight and aboveboard. He worded it in typical Buffett fashion, saying that with Berkshire's signature "where my mouth is" he had made a commitment to solidity and no one need worry about his playing games with Berkshire stocks.

In 1993, both Warren Buffett and Thomas Murphy were given walk-on parts for the ABC-TV soap opera *All My Children,* with Susan Lucci. The two men each received $300 for their acting services.

When Murphy got his check, he said, "I'm going to frame this."

Typically, Buffett had a wisecrack ready.

"I'm going to frame the stub."

CHAPTER TEN

The Sainted Seven

In a bellyaching message to his Berkshire Hathaway stockholders in 1988, Warren Buffett moaned first about the stock market that was not so responsive as it had been for the past twenty-four years; he groaned about higher corporate tax rates and a higher-priced market for the acquisition of businesses; and he mentioned negative industry conditions for three Berkshire stalwarts: Capital Cities/ABC, GEICO, and the Washington Post Company.

These last-mentioned comprised about one-half of Berkshire's net worth.

Buffett then switched tracks and began mentioning the positive elements of the Berkshire Hathaway portfolio.

He pointed out that twenty-four years had changed the stock into quite a different package. At the beginning, all the capital was invested in the vulnerable textile business. Now, much of the capital was invested in a number of exceptionally profitable businesses—what he called "the Sainted Seven." They included the *Buffalo News*, See's, Nebraska Furniture Mart, Scott Fetzer Manufacturing Group, Kirby, World Book, and Fechheimer. And, in 1988, "the Saints came marching in."

Those seven companies, Buffett explained, earned about 67 percent on average equity capital. The *Buffalo News* story has already been told in some detail. But the other six also deserve attention.

Buffett had purchased See's Candy Shops on January 2, 1972, at a price of $25 million. He acquired it through funds from Berkshire Hathaway's Blue Chip Stamps affiliate. The candy company dated back to 1921, when a seventy-one-year-old grandmother, Mary See, founded the business with almost no capital and a very limited number of pots and pans.

The purchase of See's was a Buffett-type enterprise. The story went that once he had made a deal on the price, he immediately put Charles Huggins in charge of the company, and never looked back. The agreement, he later said, was "conceived in about five minutes and never reduced to written contract—that remains unchanged to this day."

From the beginning, it was the quality of See's candies that kept the company going. The product list soon included boxed chocolates with candies like Walnut Cluster, Peanut Cluster, Almond Square, Milk Patties, Molasses Chip, and Milk Cherry.

These were produced—and still are—in the company's two primary kitchens, one in Los Angeles, the other in San Francisco. The confections are distributed through more than 200 retail stores located in twelve Western and Midwestern states and Hawaii. More than 165 stores are located in California, where the company makes 80 percent of its profits.

But the store does a bang-up job of shipping its products directly to its customers from a number of distribution centers. Many customers are out-of-staters who have visited California, discovered the stores, and now order their candies directly from the company. Of course, the candies do not sell well in the hot summer months, but the winter sales are heavy and consistent. Half the company's sales occur in the final two months of the year. The packages shipped in the winter months are gift-wrapped for perfect Christmas presents.

From the time Huggins took over management of See's, the profits have increased on a steady basis. For example, See's net income for 1981 ran at about $6 million. In 1991, ten years later, it had swelled to over $25 million. That's a quadrupling of net.

Buffett began plugging See's candies from the time he first bought the firm. But, in his typically Midwestern fashion of never overdoing anything, he limited himself from the start to eating a two-pound box of See's a month—and no more! Of course, the box was always open to everyone in the office headquarters at Kiewit Square.

The fame of See's spread far beyond Warren Buffett. In 1982, an English firm offered to buy the company from Berkshire Hathaway for $120 million in cash. But Buffett turned them down. He had too much faith in the candies himself.

For example, he reported that Americans ate 26 million pounds of See's products in 1991. The obvious thing for Buffett to do was to expand the base of the candy business past the Western and Midwestern states to embrace all the United States. But the candy business, he discovered, has always been a tricky one. He decided ultimately to keep the company lean and man, and thinned down for good service rather than expanded and apt to become corpulent and comatose.

"We've looked at dozens of ideas of how to expand," he admitted once. "And in the end we haven't found how to do it."

Buffett purchased the Nebraska Furniture Mart in 1983 for $55 million. For that price he got 80 percent of the store. It was by no means a spur-of-the-moment decision.

He had been acquainted with the store for years—it was founded in 1935, when Warren was only five years old. His mouth had always watered over the size of the business and the amount of money it made.

He knew the history of the owner and founder, Rose Blumkin, who was born Rose Gorelick in 1893 in a place near Minsk in what was then czarist Russia. The daughter of a rabbi, she never had any schooling, but helped her mother run a grocery store, baking the bread and taking care of customers.

On her own Rose learned to read and to do arithmetic so that, at thirteen, she got a job in a dry-goods store in Minsk. At sixteen, she was running the store, supervising five men. In 1914 she married Isadore Blumkin, who left for America, with Rose promising to follow.

The war stopped that. She was forced to sneak aboard a Trans-Siberian Railway train, but was halted at the Chinese frontier. She talked her way past the border and crossed Manchuria to Japan, where she got a job on a peanut boat. In six weeks she was living in Seattle.

She and her husband settled in Omaha in 1919. Isadore Blumkin ran a pawnshop and secondhand clothing store. Mrs. Blumkin sold furniture in her basement, learning to speak a kind of broken English from her kids, who picked it up at school. In 1937 Mrs. B., as she was now known, got $500 together and rented a storefront on Farnam Street. She named the store Nebraska Furniture Mart.

"Sell cheap and tell the truth!" was her motto—and her modus operandi.

She had a mouth on her, Mrs. B. "You worthless golem!" she would scream at her kids. (A "golem" was a blockhead.) "Dummy! Lazy!" Her son Louie was the opposite of his mother. Mrs. B. fired people. Louie hired them back. But he had the same business sense she had. Their method:

- Buy in volume.
- Keep expenses to a minimum.
- Pass on the savings.

The idea was to sell at about 10 percent above cost. In doing so, Mrs. B. undersold her competitors substantially—and made all the more money for her salesmanship.

Warren's wife, Susan, dealt with Mrs. B. all the time on household goods. It was Susan who got Warren interested in the store itself—especially the prices of the goods. What interested him mostly was the fact that Mrs. B. was running one competitor after another out of business.

And so Buffett made an attempt to buy the store from her.

Mrs. B. turned him down: "Too cheap." (She meant the offer, not Warren Buffett.)

But Buffett kept his eyes on things through the years. The success of the Nebraska Furniture Mart was astonishing. It was the biggest furniture store in the country, with about $100 million in annual sales. It was earning $15 million profit before taxes. In Omaha, it sold two-thirds of all the furniture sold. Some department store chains refused to open stores in Omaha because of the ominous presence of the Mart.

Finally, in 1983, Buffett had seen enough to know that he had to acquire the Mart—and Mrs. B. as well.

The scene went something like this:

BUFFETT (*walking into the Nebraska Furniture Mart*): Today is my birthday, and I want to buy your store. How much do you want for it?

MRS. B.: Sixty million dollars.

Buffett exits, then returns with the check made out.

BUFFETT *(extending the check)*: Here it is.

MRS. B.: Where are your accountants, lawyers, and investment bankers?

BUFFETT: I trust you more.

Actually, the final purchase price was $55 million, not
$60 million. The point of the story is that the actual con-
tract between these two individuals was only two pages
long. But then, Warren Buffett always favored older managers over younger ones. And Mrs. B. had a special place
in his heart.

"We find it's hard to teach a new dog old tricks," he
said once. "But we haven't had lots of problems with
people who hit the ball out of the park year after year.
Even though they're rich, they love what they do. And
nothing ever happens to our managers. We offer them
immortality."

Unfortunately, Mrs. B. did not accept immortality. In
fact, although Buffett kept bringing his friends and associates in to see the store and to meet the curmudgeonly
lady who ran it, their friendship did not continue forever.

She was almost a caricature of the self-made, self-
motivating ideal entrepreneur that Warren Buffett kept in
his mind. And therein lay the problem. It was in May
1989, some six years after he had bought the store, that
Mrs. B. got into a terrible row with her own family members about the running of the Nebraska Furniture Mart's
carpet department. What made her go ballistic was the
fact that her own people were picking on the carpet department—her favorite!

She quit. Walked out of the store. Then issued her

demands. She had never taken a vacation in her life. Everybody knew that. Warren Buffett had spread the information across the face of the globe about her work habits—her workaholic obsession, actually. Now she demanded $96,000 for unused vacation time—in cash. And she got it.

But Mrs. B. never rested. She did not wind up on that exotic island in the South Pacific. She went into business. That's right. She started *another* furniture company across the street and gave her own store a run for the money.

She called the new store Mrs. B.'s Warehouse. And it was there that she sold carpets and furniture. "Their price $104; our price $80" was a typical sign hung up in the window.

It was a sad parting of the ways for Buffett and Mrs. B., but the mixture had gotten Buffett a very good working store for his own and he had confidence in the offspring of Mrs. B., hoping they had inherited some of her grit and savvy.

Mrs. B. was the only manager Warren Buffett had left in place who eventually defected on him. But of course it was bound to be someone like Mrs. B.—a character from a novel, almost, in her approach to life.

The day before Mrs. B.'s ninety-eighth birthday—December 1, 1991—Buffett sprang a surprise visit on Mrs. B.'s Warehouse, giving her two dozen pink roses and a five-pound box of See's candy.

"He's quite a gentleman," the *Omaha World-Herald* quoted her as saying. "I do a very good business there, but it's hard to manage it," she added. "My son offered to buy me out, and I'm going to sell."

"When?"

"Time will tell. . . . I would sell only one way—if they let me work."

Warren Buffett made a fortune in his judicious purchase of Nebraska Furniture Mart. Nineteen years in textiles with Berkshire Hathaway netted him approximately as much as fifteen *months* in Mrs. B.'s furniture business.

The third important purchase, which brought in a number of the Sainted Seven companies, was that of the Scott & Fetzer Company of Cleveland, Ohio. Buffett bought it in 1986 for $410 million, comprising $320 million for the company's assets and a $90 million assumption of Scott & Fetzer debt.

Scott Fetzer, as it was called by everyone, had been on the auction block since 1984. The purchase was arranged in Chicago on October 22, 1985, and contracts were signed the following week.

The Scott Fetzer situation was a complex one from beginning to end. And complexity was what Warren Buffett and Charlie Munger did not like in their annual reports. Actually, Scott Fetzer brought in three main business for Berkshire Hathaway to run: Scott Fetzer manufacturing Group, which included more than a dozen diverse and obscure enterprises; Kirby Vacuum Cleaners of Cleveland, Ohio; and World Book. Along with these companies, there was Scott Fetzer Financial Group of Westlake and Columbus, Ohio, a company that helped customers finance Kirby and World Book Products.

The first of the rather offbeat enterprises in the manufacturing group was Campbell Hausfield/Scott Fetzer Company, which made air compressors, spray painting units, and high-pressure sprayers and washers. Another in the group, Wayne Home Equipment, sold furnace burners, and sump, utility, and sewage pumps. Other companies sold conduit fittings, roll-up awnings, appliance timing controls, ignition transformers, boat winches, cutlery, maintenance chemicals, and custom steel bodies for truck chassis.

Kirby and World Book were the best of the companies, though. Kirby's vacuum cleaners were expensive; its Generation 3 model was priced at $1,289. In consumer surveys, Kirby tended to rank first.

"It leaves the others in the dust," Buffett once said in his kidding tone.

The company had about seven hundred factory distributors. Kirby encircled the globe, with about one-third of its sales made overseas. In many countries, salesmen would still plod from door to door demonstrating vacuum cleaners—a sales method that had more or less died out in the United States.

World Book, Inc., published *Childcraft*, a children's resource; *Early World of Learning*, a preschool educational program; and annually a revised edition of the *World Book Encyclopedia*.

J. H. Hanson of the Hanson-Bellows Company in Chicago had published an encyclopedia called *The New Practical Reference Library* in the early years of the century. In order to update it and give it more marketplace appeal, he spent $150,000 on editors and rewrite men to come up with a brand-new encyclopedia, which he introduced in 1917 as *The World Book—Organized Knowledge in Story and Pictures*.

But in 1918 Hanson went broke. He sold *World Book*—what there was of it—to one of his former associates, an accountant named W. F. Quarrie. For some reason the company hit a lucky streak and was soon a flourishing enterprise.

With the surprise success of the new encyclopedia, the company began to go in for big names to byline its articles and give its overall image some pizzazz. Emily Post, the expert in etiquette, was featured. Bishop Fulton J. Sheen became a contributor. So did J. Edgar Hoover.

In 1945 the Chicago financier Marshall Field III purchased *World Book*. He planned to use the encyclopedia as the flagship of a new learning company that he had named Field Enterprises Educational Corporation. "Edu-

cation is the keystone of the democratic form of government," he once said. The *World Book*, he pointed out,
would be a key weapon in the battle for education.

Scott Fetzer bought *World Book* in 1978, and when Buffett bought Scott Fetzer, he got *World Book* with it.

The *World Book Encyclopedia* was a huge, sprawling
enterprise. Twenty million pounds of paper went into the
publication of each year's edition. The paper would
stretch 194 million feet, or about 37,000 miles, or across
the continental United States more than twelve times. For
one recent edition there were about 100 million characters
of type; it took three and a half months of press run to
complete the first printing. The presses used up seventeen
thousand gallons of ink. To produce and market the encyclopedia, the company hired five hundred employees and
used a forty-thousand-member sales force.

The effort and materials were worth every penny. Encyclopedia publishing each year was a $500 million indus-
try with four major players: *Encyclopedia Britannica,
Grolier, Collier's*, and *World Book*, and *World Book* was always the market leader. It sold more than twice as many
sets as any competitor, and sold more sets in the United
States than its top three competitors combined. The *World
Book* was in four of every ten homes that owned an encyclopedia of any kind in the United States and Canada,
and it was marketed in more than seventy countries and
was translated into many languages, including Arabic,
Chinese, Finnish, Indonesian, Japanese, Korean, Malay,
Portuguese, Spanish, Swedish, Thai, and Turkish.

It has been estimated that more than 111 million people grew up with *World Book* between 1912 and 1988. It
was also estimated that there were 12 million *World Book*
sets in use worldwide.

In June 1986, a year after Buffett bought Scott Fetzer,
Berkshire Hathaway acquired Fechheimer. Buffett snapped

up at least 84 percent of the company for a cool $46 million. The deal was a typical Buffett wheel-and-deal. Bob Heldman, a longtime Berkshire shareholder, wrote to Warren Buffett, and put the company owned by him and his brother George up for sale on the line.

The company manufactured and distributed uniforms. The Heldmans were hands-on managers known for personally opening the company's mail every day. The company had forty-three stores in twenty-two states when it was purchased. It then began expanding.

The stores went by different names throughout the country. They now are McCain Uniform Company in Birmingham and Mobile, Alabama. They are Pima Uniforms in Arizona. They are Kay Uniforms in Tennessee. They are Uniforms of Texas in Texas.

In all, in 1988, just as Warren Buffett had said, the Seven Saints came marching in.

CHAPTER ELEVEN

Berkshire Addenda

Another typical "Berkshire investment" that Warren Buffett made in the 1970s was a savings and loan company called Wesco Financial Corporation, located in California.

He had known about the company for years, having read its annual reports since the middle sixties. And he had always considered it a possible investment because of the low numbers at which it consistently traded. In the summer of 1972, for example, Wesco was on the market at a very low figure—in the teens—and Buffett decided that it was time to make some sort of move.

He bought 8 percent of its shares.

And then, quite suddenly, in January 1973, Wesco's management announced that the company was going to merge with another California savings and loan company, Financial Corporation of Santa Barbara. Buffett was silently outraged. He felt he had been sandbagged in the worst possible way.

As he saw it, Wesco was getting much the worst of the impending deal. Merging with Financial Corporation of Santa Barbara would be dissipating Wesco's funds in an inferior organization, since the combination of the two companies would be a less valuable property than each company separately. Wesco, in Buffett's view, was a much more productive company than Financial Corporation of Santa Barbara ever could be.

He knew he had to do something—and do it fast. He did not need a great deal of research to find out where to go to push the right buttons. Acting more or less as a detective, he discovered that the owner of the largest number of shares of Wesco was Elizabeth Peters, the daughter and heiress of Wesco's founders. Peters's parents had taken the savings and loan public in the late fifties, shortly after founding it, in order to get an infusion of operating cash.

Elizabeth Peters's brothers had shown neither the talent nor interest necessary to keep Wesco afloat, and so responsibility for the company had fallen on her. It turned out that she was good at managing the savings and loan; at the very least she seemed to be doing very well with it. Buffett looked carefully at the numbers and decided that she was the one he should be talking to about the future of the company.

In the seventies things looked so sour for *all* savings and loans that when Financial Corporation of Santa Barbara made its pitch for a merger agreement, Peters quite happily went for it. Then Buffett approached her directly.

Above all, he flattered her by treating her as a definite equal to him in the financial business. He told her that Wesco's merger with Financial would be a major error on Wesco's part. Peters was impressed by Buffett's argument. And, as frequently happened with people who had not met Warren Buffett before and were suddenly thrust into the aura of his compelling persona, she found herself enthralled.

As Buffett continued to explain in his own way the terms of the merger and what it would do to Wesco, Peters made up her mind. Yes, she would vote against the merger. But, she asked Buffett, if he should not be there to help her in the future, what would she do then? Who would help her? Whom could she count on for good advice?

Warren Buffett had already considered the possible hesitation on the part of Elizabeth Peters, a person who was about to come into a large honey pot of fresh money from Financial. He knew exactly how to sweeten the pot *he* was offering. Here was his solution: Berkshire Hathaway would buy a big slice of Wesco's stock. Peters would get the money she needed from him—not from Financial.

Of the 7.1 million Wesco shares outstanding, Berkshire finally bought 5.7 million of them. Most of the shares not owned by Berkshire at the end of the transaction were owned by the Peters family.

Wesco owned at least three main businesses. The first was a savings and loan bank, Mutual Savings and Loan Association of Pasadena, California. Second was a steel business, Precision Steel Warehouse, Inc., of Chicago, Illinois. Precision had its steel service centers in Franklin Park, Illinois, and Charlotte, North Carolina, along with operations in Downers Grove, Illinois. The third was later acquired: the Wesco-Financial Insurance Company of Omaha, a member of the Berkshire Hathaway Insurance Group. In addition, Wesco owned a small insurance agency, WSC Insurance Agency, in Pasadena.

To tie it all together in a neat Buffett-style package, Wesco's Mutual Savings and Loan Association was located right across the street from a See's candy shop in the Plaza Pasadena shopping center. And Wesco's headquarters was not far from Cypress Insurance Corporation, of Pasadena, one of Berkshire's insurance businesses, which dealt regularly with Wes-FIC, which reinsured about half the business of Cypress.

By the time the contracts were signed and the transaction was completed, Berkshire, through Blue Chip

Stamps, owned about 80.1 percent of Wesco Financial Corporation.

After its acquisition by Berkshire in 1972, Wesco became known as a very steady part of Berkshire Hathaway, though in no way a spectacular part. As for acquiring new companies, or as for fast growth, Warren Buffett said at the 1986 Berkshire meeting that looking for companies to acquire could be compared to a man's search for a wife or a woman's search for a husband.

"You can thoughtfully establish certain qualities you'd like her to have, an then all of a sudden, you meet someone and you do it."

Later, Wesco would own 80 percent of the stock of New American Electrical Corporation, of Anaheim, California, purchased in 1988 for $8.2 million. The other 20 percent was owned by New American Electrical's chief executive officer, Glen Mitchel.

In the long run, Wesco consistently paid out a very steady and reliable dividend every year, accounting for about 15 percent of Berkshire's money annually. Not a bad percentage at all!

Another of Berkshire's important investments was made in 1988, when Warren Buffett purchased 7.2 million shares of stock—4 percent of the total, all he was allowed—in the Federal Home Loan Mortgage Corporation, or "Freddie Mac," with $71.7 million of Wesco's money.

Freddie Mac is the cousin of "Fannie Mae," the Federal National Mortgage Association. Both are quasi corporations established to help people borrow money to build homes.

Freddie Mac, chartered by Congress in 1970, was created to purchase residential mortgages from money lenders, guaranteeing the mortgages against default. After buying the mortgages it packaged them as securities and sold them to investors, including many savings and loan companies.

From 1970 through 1987, the market for residential mortgages grew to the tune of a compound annual rate of more than 13 percent and never at less than 5.5 percent a year. But what made Freddie Mac and Fannie Mae the powerhouses they were was the fact that they had virtually no competition. They controlled 90 percent of the market.

It was one government business that *worked*.

As Warren Buffett said about the duopoly of Freddie Mac and Fannie Mae: "It's the next best thing to a monopoly."

Warren Buffett could never say enough good things about Freddie Mac. "Freddie Mac is a triple dip," he noted. "You've got a low price/earnings ratio on a company with a terrific record. You've got growing earnings. And you have a stock that is bound to become much better known to equity investors."

Over twenty-five-odd years of operation, Freddie Mac financed one in eight of all American homes, including more than 700,000 apartment units. Yet about 97 percent of the company's business dealt with single-family home mortgages. So only about one-third of conventional residential mortgages were securitized—and that had left plenty of room for the growth of Freddie Mac.

There was another plus to Freddie Mac: its return on equity usually averaged more than twice Fannie Mae's. Also, Freddie Mac's delinquency rate for conventional fixed-rate singe-family mortgages was a mere 0.4 percent of its $230 billion portfolio. In comparision, Fannie Mae had delinquencies of 1.1 percent.

Freddie Mac could minimize its exposure to interest-rate spikes, which hurt mortgage bankers, simply by raising their cost of money while lowering the price of mortgages in the secondary market. Freddie Mac kept only $15 billion worth of mortgages on the balance sheet; Fannie Mae kept $102 million.

In the eighties, Berkshire Hathaway sold its shares of Fannie Mae, and put the money into more Freddie Macs. The rationale was simple: buy as many Freddie Macs as possible—limited, of course, by the 4 percent ceiling of Freddie Macs mandated in the original charter.

Nevertheless, in early 1990, after Buffett had made the investment in the Freddie Mac stock at a cost per share of about $30, it suddenly began to sink fast, along with the free-falling real estate market of the same year.

At the low of 1990, the stock had lost two-thirds of its value from its 1989 peak and was trading on an insubstantial price/earnings ratio of about 5 times earnings. Wesco's stock sank quickly, and the stock market echoed the troubles by sinking in the middle of 1990.

But Freddie Mac's single-family home mortgage business remained strong. It was the apartment-backed mortgage business—as in New York—that suffered the most. However, in 1991 the market steadied up and Freddie Mac rebounded.

In March 1992 there was good news once again for Freddie Mac. The real estate crisis seemed to have abated. The company proposed a 3–for–1 stock split and a 14 percent dividend increase. Now, with the split in stock, Berkshire acquired about 75 million shares of Freddie Mac.

With more to come in the future.

An astute investor like Warren Buffett would be expected never to have taken a flier at the junk bonds issued during the 1980s. And yet, oddly enough, Buffett did just that—though there *were* mitigating circumstances. And there were very good reasons for his decision to trade in junk for the time being.

Everyone had heard the term "junk bond," but very

few people not connected directly to Wall Street knew exactly what one was. The pejorative "junk" established that this type of bond was no good. But what could be "no good" about a bond?

Actually, the real term for a junk bond was a "high-yield bond." Such a bond was called "high-yield" because it paid high interest rates—usually in double-digit figures. The high-yield bond became extremely popular in the eighties when leveraged buyouts and takeovers were the talk—and the action—on Wall Street.

Junk bonds paid high interest rates because the people issuing them had to have a lot of money very quickly, usually in order to finance the expensive buyout of a firm that was having trouble with its cash flow. But the bonds were "junk" because they were very risky; after all, the people who issued them were saddled with quick extra debt that they might not be able to pay off at will. It was not unusual for the issuers of these high-interest bonds to find themselves in the middle of high debts and unable to trade anymore.

All through the eighties, Warren Buffet had lived by a saying he became famous for:

"Junk bonds will one day live up to their name."

And yet in 1989 Buffett began to buy up RJR (R. J. Reynolds) bonds—junk bonds for sure.

In his 1990 Berkshire Hathaway annual report, Buffett was still railing against the typical junk bonds that were all over the marketplace. The way he put it was vintage Buffett:

"The only time to buy these bonds is on a day with no 'y' in it."

However, in spite of his adamant dislike of junk bonds, he reported, he was exploring the field to see if some of them might be valuable to him—and, sure enough, he'd found one. It was RJR Nabisco and it looked very good.

He said that he still did not like junk bonds per se, and found most of them very unattractive. Besides that, junk bonds had ruined many a decent corporation. He was still looking for the right thing, and might certainly buy it, should it prove worthy.

During the time he was writing that report, Warren was, in fact, picking up RJR bonds. But no one was aware of what he was doing until the news of his actions came out in the 1991 Berkshire annual report. It was not until page 17 that Buffett mentioned junk bonds at all, and here he talked about RJR Nabisco. He then confessed that he had $440 million invested at the end of 1990 in RJR Nabisco, an amount that was about market value. And the stock at that point had just risen in value.

At first it appeared Buffett had waited just a trifle too long to pick up the RJR bonds. What happened happened quickly. R. J. Reynolds/Nabisco was actually cutting back at its home base, trying to stanch the flow of blood. And things seemed to be working out. Quite abruptly, on May 3, 1991, RJR management held a press conference and said that RJR was retiring most of the junk bonds used to refinance its operations. It had raised the money in a stock offering. Now Reynolds said it would redeem the junk bonds at face value—and these were bonds that Warren had purchased at a deep discount.

The money came in and Buffett once again discovered that he had made a huge and quick profit on a dubious enterprise at best. But was it just luck? He couldn't always be so right, could he?

At the end of the year 1991 Berkshire held more than $1 billion in junk bonds not only from RJR, but from Washington Public Power System and ACF Industries as well.

It was in the late eighties that Buffett purchased an important Omaha jewelry store. This one was Borsheim's, named after its founder, Louis Borsheim. The company had been started back in 1870. It had a nice run through the turn of the century, and was still quite stable in 1948, when it was purchased by Louis Friedman and his wife, Rebecca.

But as with many of Buffett's ventures, there was a clandestine tie-in here. Rebecca Friedman was the former Rebecca Blumkin, the sister of Rose Blumkin of Nebraska Furniture Mart fame. The store was run by Ike Friedman, Louis and Rebecca's son, and Ike's son Alan; plus two sons-in-law, Donald Yale and Marvin Cohn.

Of course Buffett knew the Friedmans, and knew of the Friedmans' tie to Rose Blumkin. It was in 1989 that Buffett began to get interested in Borsheim's as a possible acquisition. He visited the store and asked quietly if it might be for sale.

Ike Friedman was willing. It was he who made the deal with Buffett. He reported later that the negotiations were over in a half hour. Buffett's questions, Friedman recalled, were typical of the man:

- What are sales?
- What's the annual net increase in sales?
- What's in inventory?
- What's the debt?
- Are you willing to stay on?

Friedman answered the questions that he could answer: the debt was zero, and yes, he would stay. And that was it. Buffett bought 80 percent of the business. The price was determined, and the papers were made up.

As usual, Buffett paid cash.

Buffett did discuss with Friedman the ease with which the negotiations had proceeded. "Ike," he said, "there are only a handful of people I do business with this way. And none of them is a Fortune 500 company."

The sale price was kept secret, but was rumored to have been about $60 million. Once the store changed owners, absolutely nothing else was altered. It was Buffett who talked to Donald Yale.

"Now, forget that it happened, and just keep doing what you are doing."

Donald Yale: "There was no discussion of future growth and absolutely no discussion of changing our way of making decisions, planning expansion, or bringing in additional profits. He made it very clear that he was not in this as a quick-return deal."

And so Borsheim's joined that select group of companies that Buffett trusted to operate correctly as they had always operated before he put up the purchase money. No change would be necessary here. Everything was perfect as it was.

In fact, the stare was one of the biggest independent jewelry stores in the United States. It employed two hundred people full-time and had fifty to seventy-five extras during the Christmas season and other peak holidays.

The company did not let its employees work on a commission per sales basis. Management had always felt that if the salesperson was totally involved in making money while making a sale, he or she might well think it was more important to make that personal sale than to serve the customer.

In 1986 the store expanded fivefold. It moved from its 6,800-square-foot location to a new site in the Regency Fashion Court Mall, in a 37,000-square-foot area.

Borsheim's claimed that more than half the jewelry sold in Omaha, Nebraska, was sold from the store itself. But unlike most places of business that depended upon people who came in to do their shopping, Borsheim's conducted almost 40 percent of its jewelry business outside the store—usually by telephone or even by mail from catalogs sent to the customers.

When Ike Friedman died on September 12, 1991, Donald Yale was named president and chief executive officer of Borsheim's. Marvin Cohn was named executive vice president. Buffett became chairman of the board. Even then, he didn't change a thing. As Buffett might have said: Don't fix what isn't broke.

CHAPTER TWELVE

Coca-Cola

For years the picture of Warren Buffett sipping Pepsi-Cola from a bottle and munching a hamburger had been sufficient to produce the proper public image of the down-to-earth Midwestern small-businessman and decent citizen—the kind of guy Warren Buffett wanted to be considered.

But in 1985 that picture would develop a new dimension: Warren Buffett, shrewd and canny investor.

A bit of history is now in order for those interested in the hows and whys of success in the business world. And it is necessary to go way back into the nineteenth century—May 8, 1886, to be exact—to view that history in the making. For that was the day when a Georgia pharmacist, Dr. John Styth Pemberton, poured a number of ingredients into a three-legged brass pot in the backyard of his Atlanta home.

He had concocted a beverage made from sugar, some spices, and extracts of flavor from the kola nut and the coca leaf. Then he'd carbonized the drink.

Pemberton liked the tangy taste of the drink itself. It stirred the inside of his mouth when he took a full swig.

Besides that, it was a syrupy mixture, but not *too* sticky.
And there was an underlying *exotic* flavor apparently
caused by the mixture of the coca leaf and the kola nut.
It would do.

Atlanta, Georgia, lay in a countryside that was apt to
overheat in the summer, and sometimes in the spring and
fall as well. And a pharmacy's friendly soda fountain was
just the place to sell drinks to people who were trying to
escape the hot sun for a bit of refreshment.

Served with ice in it, Pemberton thought, this would
be a drink that might prove marketable in Atlanta.

The very next year he filed a patent for the product.
After huddling with friends and family, and paying attention especially to his bookkeeper, Frank M. Robinson, he
had decided to call the artificial beverage just what it was:
part coca leaf and part kola nut. Hence, as Robinson saw
it, "Coca-Kola."

The sound was good, the two men decided, but something bothered Robinson about the juxtaposition of the *C*
and the *K*. Why couldn't they have named the kola tree
a *cola* tree? Why not, indeed? Then, you could have a
drink called "Coca-Cola." *That* would be absolutely right.
So after thinking it over, the two men figured that *they'd*
spell it with two Cs. Robinson was particularly pleased.

First, he was a fanatic for alliteration. The two hard
C sounds would also be memorable, as hard consonants
so often are. By combining the named of the two basic
ingredients of the drink into a hyphenated entity—Coca-
Cola—Robinson had three hard Cs to brag about. The
name stuck in the mind, too.

Pemberton loved it. It had *something*. He let Robinson,
who had a better handwriting than he did, fool around
with the name just a bit. The bookkeeper Robinson had
perfected a version of the flowing, memorable Spencerian
script that was so popular in America at that time. And

it was he who wrote out the very first "Coca-Cola" for the patent office's files.

Meanwhile, Pemberton began serving the beverage at his pharmacy to thirsty Atlantans. It went over pretty well. Nothing smashing. But even in the winter months people began to form a habit of dropping by Pemberton's to have a "Coca-Cola" on the way home.

The new beverage was not marketed in a bottle at all. It was simply mixed at the soda fountain. First the basic syrup, made from Pemberton's "secret formula," was squirted in the glass, and then the carbonated water was added to start the beverage fizzing.

Even with this local popularity, the beverage did not get off to a triumphant start. The records later showed that in 1886, the year Pemberton began selling it at his store, sales averaged about nine drinks a day.

The nonsuccess of the newly concocted "Coca-Cola" was not lost on other businessmen around the area. Everyone liked the beverage, but it was hard to get the stuff promoted. And advertising cost a lot of money.

A man named Asa Griggs Candler became interested in buying the rights to the beverage, lock, stock, and barrel, from Pemberton. In 1891, Pemberton signed over the rights to Coca-Cola for a measly $2,300—measly only in terms of today's dollar. In Pemberton's book, Candler was buying a pig in a poke, a pig that Pemberton, to fracture the metaphor, had been unable to teach any new tricks— and good luck to Candler!

Candler began by bottling the beverage so that it didn't need to be sold exclusively at a soda fountain. He started advertising it everywhere he could think of. By 1895, Coca-Cola was on sale—both as a syrup to be served with carbonated water and as a bottled beverage—in every state and territory in the union.

With the high-powered advertising, the logo soon

caught on. People began asking for Coca-Cola at soda fountains.

Candler knew he had a winner with the now-famous logo. And he began promoting Coca-Cola mercilessly— on calendars, clocks, fans, and every novelty he could get hold of—to tell the public about this marvelous new drink.

Pretty soon Coca-Cola was known familiarly as simply "Coke." That incarnation set off negative vibrations in some wary customers. Cocaine was an addictive drug at the time, known primarily *as* "coke." However, the very similarity may have *helped* rather than hurt Coca-Cola's popularity. Some customers would stroll up to a soda fountain, sit down, and order a "dope."

Soda jerks all over the country began experimenting with the drink. They would add other flavored syrups to the original Coca-Cola formula, and shoot the concoction full of carbonated water. And so were born numerous variations on Coke—cherry Coke, lemon Coke, raspberry Coke, and so on.

Even the design of the bottle spoke of deliberate marketing. Bottles for beverages in those days were of various shapes and sizes. It was the genius of the makers of Coca-Cola to keep the shape of the bottle always in the public eye. Its distinctive curve from the neck down—some said it approximated the silhouette of a shapely woman—was instantly recognizable and became as much a part of Coca-Cola as the distinctive logo.

By 1919 the company was reaping millions in profit every year. It became such a tremendous marketing success that other companies began imitating Coca-Cola, but none of them ever seemed to equal Coke in popularity. Even Pepsi-Cola, which came later, based its sales appeal on the *amount* of beverage rather than the quality.

Coke's much smaller bottle would remain that size for years.

The company was so successful at the end of World War I that a group of investors under the leadership of Ernest Woodruff paid $25 million for all rights to Coca-Cola. Soon enough, in 1923, Woodruff's son, Robert W. Woodruff, became president. And this man proved to be the pilot of the company for at least six decades—right through the crucial middle years of the twentieth century.

Woodruff was responsible for a number of extremely successful marketing ploys. One of them was the six-pack, which spread to every other beverage company in the country almost instantaneously. He was also a genius at promoting the beverage with picturesque displays and all kinds of marketing techniques. And he tested out numerous kinds of vending and dispensing equipment—all developed to sell Coca-Cola.

It was under Woodruff that Coca-Cola became a worldwide institution—even in Russia! But it was Woodruff's activities during World War II that gave Coca-Cola a toehold in many a foreign land, to be exploited after the war.

As the United States entered World War II in 1941, Woodruff vowed that "every man in uniform gets a bottle of Coca-Cola for five cents, wherever he is and whatever it costs the company."

He was true to his word. The presence of Coca-Cola for the troops to buy no matter where they were was a tremendous morale booster. And indeed in foreign countries, whose people had never heard of Coca-Cola until the Yanks came, Coke took hold quickly and became a popular drink that could not be ignored.

When the U.S. troops eventually pulled out, there were enough people now accustomed to their Coca-Cola diet that it was easy for the company to start up bottling operations in select countries overseas. Coca-Cola was, in fact, one of the obvious signs of the presence of Americans in any given area.

The hit song "Rum and Coca-Cola," recorded by the Andrews Sisters and released toward the end of hostilities, did not hurt Coke's popularity anywhere at all, either. *Yank Magazine* had a cartoon of an obviously hungover G.I. on the morning after, drinking Coke from a bottle and saying something like this: "Hey, without all that other crud in it, this stuff ain't half bad!"

The postwar world was now Coca-Cola's stamping ground—the entire postwar world. And yet in the 1970s, after a series of phenomenal surges, the company seemed to be drifting. The foreign bottling companies were not particularly profitable over the long haul, since many of the owners were not good at marketing their product.

But profits continued to rise and the company expanded into other businesses. It got into the wine business, and even bottled water. In fact, some units manufactured steam boilers and pasta, of all things. It even marketed tea and coffee. But since the bottom line continued to be appealing, there were no big changes made.

Nevertheless, getting into these odd businesses was the same as squandering good cash. The chief executive, J. Paul Austin, was running a ship that was now seemingly adrift. The bottom line told the story: in the midseventies, the annual return on Coca-Cola stock was a tiny 1 percent.

Robert C. Goizueta took over in 1981. It was he who hired Donald Keough, who in years past had lived right across the street from Warren Buffett in Omaha. Goizueta did not realize he was following a dangerous pattern in diversifying like his predecessor, and he purchased Columbia Pictures, a not-too-successful studio left over from the golden age of motion pictures in the 1930s.

In the eighties the battle began between the two giants: Coca-Cola and Pepsi-Cola. Pepsi had never really won the battle with Coke. Now it decided that it had to do so or get out of the business entirely. The people at

Coca-Cola panicked. Goizueta wanted action. And it was under his aegis that in 1985 Coca-Cola abandoned its tried-and-true formula of a hundred years and unveiled the "New Coke."

The New Coke became the New Joke in the business world. Everybody else was laughing—but not Coca-Cola. And when the company brass realized that they had practically killed the goose that laid the golden egg, the company immediately began to look in upon itself.

The point was, the New Coke was sweeter than the original Coke, but it was thinner and simply did not pack the old wallop that true Coke drinkers loved. Goizueta was no fool. He knew that he had to market the old Coke as well as the New Coke. And perhaps some new mixes.

In the end, with the "Classic Coke" (as it came to be called after its return by popular demand) alongside the New Coke, the company found that it had *increased*, not decreased, its earnings. The fiasco had turned out to be a blessing in disguise. The company even came out with a bottled Cherry Coke, which proved to be a success as well.

Now Goizueta began looking over all the claptrap that the Coca-Cola Company had bought up during its drifting, acquiring years. And he began selling off everything that had nothing to do with beverages. Goizueta was the right man for that job. He had been born in Cuba, the son of a sugar baron, and he had started work at a bottling plant in Havana. He realized that he should have been paying more attention to Coca-Cola's bottling problems around the globe instead of worrying so much about domestic problems with the company.

Soon the company was engaged in a worldwide battle against local beverage companies and in some cases against Pepsi-Cola, which was trying to work its way into foreign locales. Coca-Cola was beginning to win new converts.

Goizueta realized that cash was coming in from his sale of the many companies that Coca-Cola had bought in the seventies. And he could see Coca-Cola successfully beating other beverages all over the world. The company was making money. So Goizueta did what his predecessor had not done: he began to buy back Coca-Cola stock in big hunks.

This move appealed to Warren Buffett. He realized that Goizueta was a man after his own heart. By 1985, Buffett was studying the market carefully. He found out that from 1984 to 1987, the total number of gallons of Coca-Cola sold overseas rose 34 percent. And the profit margin on each gallon rose, too—from 22 percent to 27 percent. Coca-Cola was getting a double profit, thanks to its struggles with the local competition overseas.

Other signs were equally good. Buffett found that in 1984, 52 percent of the company's money was earned overseas. However, by 1987, some 75 percent of its income was on a global basis. And there were black holes in the marketing heavens—places that had not even *started* to introduce cola drinking.

By 1988, Coca-Cola was trading at thirteen times its expected 1989 earnings—or about 15 percent above the average stock.

"I felt as sure of the margin of safety with Coke as when I bought Union Street Railway at 40 percent of net cash," Warren Buffett told a group at Columbia University. "In both cases you're getting more than you're paying for. It's just that one was easier to spot."

It was easy for him to pack all of Coke's virtues into one short sentence:

"If you gave me $100 billion and said take away the soft drink leadership of Coca-Cola in the world, I'd give it back to you and say it can't be done."

Donald Keough, president of Coca-Cola, called up Warren Buffett sometime in 1988 or '89 and teased him:

"Warren, are you buying a share or two of Coca-Cola stock?" Buffet said yes, and he said it enthusiastically.

Between 1985 and 1989—especially at the end of 1988—Warren was grabbing up as many shares of Coca-Cola as he could possibly get. And he was buying them as secretly as he could. He was good at it: nothing leaked out between September 1988 and March 1989 about the enormous number of shares he was acquiring. The timing was crucial, since these were the months when Berkshire was not required to report any acquisitions of that size—from September 30 until the annual report in late March.

Then, the bombshell burst. On the afternoon of March 15, 1989, there was a brief announcement over the Dow Jones newswire that Berkshire had acquired 6.3 percent of the stock of the Coca-Cola Company. It was worth over a billion dollars of Coca-Cola's stock.

"I wish we had bought more," Buffett said later.

In the next Berkshire Hathaway annual report, in 1989, Warren Buffett included a self-deprecatory statement about the speed with which he had decided to buy Coca-Cola stock.

He said he went back to his own roots and realized that it was either 1935 or 1936 when he had drunk his first Coca-Cola. And then he began merchandising the beverage. He bought Cokes at the store for six for twenty-five cents, and sold them for five cents each. He always knew Coca-Cola was a product he could sell easily. It was an attractive commodity.

Then for fifty-two years he watched Coca-Cola spread all over the globe, and finally, in the summer of 1988, he decided that he should begin buying Coke. He promised his stockholders in typical tongue-in-cheek fashion that in the future his response time to an attractive idea would be "slashed to well under fifty years."

The size of Buffett's investment in Coca-Cola was huge. It came to $1,023,920,000. With that amount of money he purchased 23,350,000 shares of Coca-Cola stock. Subsequently, the stock split 2 for 1 in 1990 and again in 1992. Berkshire Hathaway then owned an incredible 93,400,000 shares of Coke.

Buffett was elated over the success of his purchase of Coca-Cola stock. He claimed to a reporter that purchasing that much of the company was "the ultimate case of putting your money where your mouth is."

Always the joker.

Warren Buffett also elaborated on the whys and wherefores of purchasing that much Coke. He said it had a lot to do with the fact that he knew what a Coca-Cola was. Since he could understand what it was and why it was easy to sell, it was a company that he liked. He said he did not know what a transistor was but he did know what a Coke was. He was going to stick to companies that made things he understood.

One journalist suggested that Buffett's purchase of the Coca-Cola stock was a protection against a possible recession.

"There could be ten recessions between now and the time we sell our Coke stock," Buffett responded. "Our favorite holding period is forever."

The only company owning more of Coca-Cola from the outside was SunTrust Banks, Inc., which had slightly more than 10 percent of the stock. The bank owned about 2 percent and the other 8 percent was in fiduciary accounts. SunTrust, incidentally, had in its vault the only written copy of the Coke formula.

Buffett had called Coca-Cola "the most valuable franchise in the world."

It was, in the end, the *value* of Coca-Cola that Warren Buffett actually wanted. And he did everything he could do to get it. Of course, there were other reasons, too. When a reporter asked him why he opted to purchase Coca-Cola, he equated his interest to that of marrying a girl. Was it her eyes? Her personality? Her voice? No. It was a whole lot of things. But they added up to having a crush on Coca-Cola just like having a crush on a girl.

In addition, there was a kind of certainty about Coca-Cola—not just a whim. Buffett knew that management at Coca-Cola would still be pushing hard in the years to come and the stocks would be going up, not down. It was a kind of feeling that he had about certain products, and certainly Coke was one of them. Not only would management be pushing, but the product itself was a good one—one that would not change over the years. It would always be there, doing a lot more business in the future than it was doing now.

Buffett's purchase of Coca-Cola stock rejuvenated Berkshire Hathaway stock in a way that was startling and thoroughly unexpected. At the time of the purchase, the company was trading at $4,800 a share. Six months later, it had risen 66 percent, and was selling at $8,000.

Warren Buffett was suddenly worth $3.8 billion. And he was also a changed being: not just an ex–Pepsi-Cola fan, but a total Coca-Cola partisan. He acquired a mountain of trivia about Coca-Cola and could recite the details to anyone within earshot.

He could call off the sales here and there and the growth rates. He could give the per capitas in countries around the world. And he could dissect a can of Coke according to its financial ingredients.

He reported that he got a rush just from seeing the red-and-white banner above the product in a store, and could feel excited in knowing that people were drinking the product at that very moment anywhere in the world. He knew the exact bottom line: a penny of profit on each eight-ounce serving, 700 million servings a day, 250 billion a year.

Whew!

CHAPTER THIRTEEN

Gillette, USAir, Champion International

The Coca-Cola deal had sharpened Warren Buffett's appetite for acquiring firms with international growth already established, or at least with a potential for international expansion. He had the cash to make the deals, and in his case having the cash was equivalent to a small boy's having a handful of money burning a hole in his pocket.

Buffett expressed it differently.

"There is an itch that comes about," was the way he put it, "and I get it, I confess. There is an itch to do things, particularly when you haven't done anything in a while."

At the time he said it he actually was "doing things" with Coca-Cola, but he was not talking about those things, except in veiled references. But his activities certainly explained a lot about his frame of mind concerning investment in the late eighties.

There was the big deal with Coca-Cola—a deal that was monumental in Warren Buffett's life. And right on top of it there were three more big deals that he put together almost simultaneously. He paid $1.3 billion for these, but he had the money and he felt that he had to do something with it.

The three deals?

1. Gillette
2. USAir
3. Champion International

It was late in 1989 when he put together the Gillette deal, purchasing $600 million worth of Gillette's 8.75 percent convertible preferred stock. The stock traded at about $41 a share at the time. The preferred was convertible after two years into 12 million shares at $50 a share.

The Gillette Company was founded in 1901. A salesman for Crown Cork & Seal Company named King Camp Gillette was always grousing to his boss about getting into some kind of business for himself, but not knowing exactly how to go about it.

As the story went, his boss, William Painter, got tired of hearing him squawking, and gave him a bit of advice right off the top of the head:

"Why don't you invent something that is thrown away, once used, and customers will have to come for more?"

Gillette didn't think much of the idea, because it really wasn't an idea at all; it was a concept. What he wanted were the details of an idea—the physical details of a viable product. But Painter's words kept echoing in his mind, and one morning in 1895 as he stood shaving himself in the mirror, the entire idea of a razor with disposable blades flashed through his mind, detail by detail:

- The way a blade could be fastened into a holder
- The idea of sharpening the opposite edges of a thin piece of steel
- The plates to fasten the blade to a handle

"All this came more in pictures than conscious thought," Gillette recalled, "as though the razor were already a finished thing, and held before my eyes. I stood there before the mirror in a trance of joy."

He dashed off a letter to his wife, who was visiting relatives in Ohio. "I've got it!" he wrote. "Our fortune is made!"

Essentially, he was right. But the trials and tribulations of getting his product on the market were all ahead of him. The main part of his success depended on his attitude. As he expressed it: "I believed in it with all my heart."

In 1901 Gillette founded a company in his own name and finally began marketing Gillette safety razors in a packet containing a handle and twenty blades for $5. The company went on to achieve monumental success. Gillette was not quite so lucky. For all that he had accomplished, he died broke in 1932 as a result of bad management of money and a number of accumulating debts in the 1920s.

The company had its up and downs over the years, too, but its razor was certainly a breakthrough in the marketplace as well as one for men all over the world, those who wore beards as well as those who were clean-shaven. In the era before the electric shaver came along, the safety razor, as it was called (because you couldn't slash your throat with it the way you could with a straight razor), became the mainstay of males all over the world.

Little experimentation needed to be done on the razor in its first fifty or sixty years of existence. In 1960, however, the company improved the quality of shaving by applying a silicone coating to the cutting edge of the blade. Then, in 1971, the company developed twin-blade shaving, and later refined it with the Atra pivoting head twin-blade system in 1977 and the Atra Plus in 1985. In 1990 the company launched the Sensor, a razor that could continuously "sense" the contours of the face and adjust the blade for a close, smooth shave.

Gillette bought the Papermate Pen Company in 1955,

and followed up that purchase in 1987 with the acquisition of the Waterman Pen Company of France. Gillette marketed these pens as writing instruments of superior craftsmanship.

The company made forays into the cosmetics and toiletries business. It produced shave creams, deodorants, antiperspirants, shampoos, conditioners, hair sprays, styling aids, ethnic hair-care products, home permanents, and bath and skin-care products. Figures show that Gillette owned 17 percent of the $1.6 billion U.S. deodorant market, second only to Procter & Gamble Company's 31.5 percent market share.

The development of the electric razor in the 1960s changed the entire picture for the safety razor market. Gillette came up with its own Flex Control electric razor. Then a swivel-headed razor appeared, manufactured by Braun, and sold only in Europe. In 1967, Gillette purchased Braun for $64 million. Braun was selling $1 billion a year in the early nineties.

Gillette than moved into the dental care area, developing an automatic toothbrush in its Oral-B division—a brush that was so successful that many dentists recommended it to their patients.

The company never gave up its lead as the biggest marketer of blades and razors in North America and in most other areas of the globe. The current company, more or less stabilized in 1975 by the ascension of Coleman C. Mockler as CEO, went through a bad period of economic readjustment in the 1980s.

During its down period, Gillette was the target of two takeover bids. One was generated by Ronald Perelman, Revlon's head, in 1986. The other was instigated by the now defunct Coniston Partners in 1988. Mockler wisely restructured the company, reducing the workforce and selling off units of the company that were unable to compete gracefully. During that cleanup period, Gillette

bought back almost 30 percent of its common stock, paying off its debts promptly. It could do so easily because
of the company's excellent cash flow.

The Gillette deal was all Warren Buffett's idea. He
knew Gillette was being hounded by takeover pirates, and
he knew Gillette was a sound company. It was so good
that he wanted to own part of it. And so he proposed a
quid pro quo to Joseph J. Sisco, a member of Gillette's
board, whom he knew. What he proposed was "an equity
issue that might make sense." He would get Gillette stock;
Gillette would get cash to help stave off the arbitrageurs.
The issue did make sense. The papers were signed in
July 1989.

"Gillette is synonymous with highly successful international consumer marketing and is exactly the sort of
business in which we like to invest for the long term."
So said Warren Buffett at the time the preferred stock
purchase was made.

Newsday columnist Allan Sloan pointed out that Gillette was immediately worth about $40 million more than
Buffett paid for it. But other factors made it even more
worthwhile. Gillette's introduction of the Sensor razor
turned out to be an unqualified success. The company's
stock zoomed up. Even the Persian Gulf War, which put a
crimp in stock market values overall, turned out to be only
a minor setback. On February 21, 1991, Gillette announced
a 2-for-1 split and a rise in dividends. With the split, Berkshire wound up with 24 million shares of common stock.

In the end, Gillette turned out to be a fantastically
successful investment. Warren Buffett wound up with a
solid stake in an irreplaceable consumer products company with an absolutely wonderful brand name.

And now for the bad news.

The results of Warren Buffett's restlessness included
an investment in US Airways Group, Inc., of $358 mil-

lion—or about 12 percent of the company's stock—on August 7, 1989.

USAir had a checkered past. It began in the East as Allegheny Airlines. Then it bought Mohawk Airlines in 1972, combining with it. It was big enough then to operate out of a hub in Pittsburgh in 1978. In the early 1980s, USAir was sailing right along.

Then, in 1987, it acquired two more airlines, Pacific Southwest Airlines and Piedmont Aviation, Inc. The acquisitions made USAir the nation's fourth-largest airline. However, because most of its flights were short hops—it was basically a commuter airline—it cost more to operate than an airline depending on long hops. Because it was operating at a high cost it could not upgrade its planes, and continued to operate with the aged crates it should have retired long ago.

The company president, Ed Colodny, stated in his 1989 annual report that the year was a hard one for a number of isolated reasons. One of them was the problem of merging all his airlines into one. Another was the fact that the planes, operating short routes and flying on tight schedules, were old and frequently came in late, throwing the tight schedules out of whack all down the line. Baggage got lost in the confusion of transfers from one plane to another.

And then there was the competition. On the West Coast everybody—American Airlines, United Airlines, Delta Airlines, Southwest Airlines—ganged up on USAir. The competition vitiated USAir. It didn't help matters that the air fares had to go down or the number of paying passengers would decline. It was catch-22 all the way.

And then something that had absolutely nothing to do with flying in the United States occurred, and it flattened USAir. Iraq invaded Kuwait on August 2, 1990. That caused the oil business to go into a kind of cardiac arrest. Prices of crude soared. USAir posted a loss of $454 million that year alone. There was nowhere the airline could cut its overhead. And oil was going up, up, and up. There was no relief in sight.

Colodny blamed 1990's shortfall on a drop-off in flying traffic due to a weak national economy, huge increases in the price of jet fuel, and an unrealistic expectation of fare discounting. And he saw no way that these problems could be resolved.

The company had to furlough seven thousand employees—14 percent of the workforce. Purchase orders for new planes to replace the ancient ones had to be postponed. The routes had to be sharply reduced. USAir was too big to be a regional airline, and it was too small to compete with the big-time carriers.

Eastern Airlines went belly-up. Couldn't USAir go bankrupt and save itself from all the debts it had rung up?

At the 1991 Berkshire meeting, Warren Buffett explained why it could not do the obvious—that is, why USAir could not go bankrupt. He said that once an airline did that, it became free of all debts. He cited Eastern. Bankrupted, Eastern picked up hundreds of millions of dollars by selling off almost everything it owned in the way of gates and other physical assets. USAir, of course, was unable to compete with Eastern's debt-free status.

Nevertheless, Buffett was playing the sanguine game: the game that lays it all out to be seen, and pretends that everything is hunky-dory. "There are no plans," he told the *Washington Post*, "just to be an investor for ten years or longer. We think when you've got an able management, they should have time to play out their hand."

Was he being simply and thoughtfully optimistic? Or was he trying to put a good face on a very bad situation? See for yourself how he handled the next few years of "no plans." Here are some notes from Berkshire's 1996 report:

In the 1990–94 period, USAir lost about $2.4 billion, a performance that wiped out the book equity of its common stock. The company paid its dividends, but in 1994 payment was suspended. Warren tried to unload the shares at 50 percent of face value.

"Fortunately," he wrote later on, "I was unsuccessful."

He also tried to unload the stock for $335 million in 1995, but that ploy did not succeed, either. In 1996 the preferred stock had again worked its way up to par value of $358, give or take a bit. And so by failing to sell off his stock, Warren Buffett again had done the right thing in the long run. But he would never let himself off the hook.

Characteristically, in the 1996 annual report he wrote that a friend had taken him to task for being a damned fool. If Buffett was so rich, the friend had added, why wasn't he smart? Buffett confessed that after he had reviewed his performance with USAir, he'd concluded that his friend had a good point.

Buffett could be merciless when he was taking potshots at himself. In the 1996 annual report for Berkshire, he inserted an old joke in its proper place:

Richard Branson, the owner of Virgin Atlantic Airways, was once asked how to become a millionaire. "There's really nothing to it," Branson replied. "Start as a billionaire and then buy an airline."

So much for Buffett's troubles with USAir.

The third 1989 deal was the Champion International one. On December 5, 1989, Buffett purchased an 8 percent preferred stock stake in Champion International, the huge forest-products company based in Stamford, Connecticut. At the time, Georgia-Pacific had launched a leveraged assault on Great Northern Nekoosa.

Andrew C. Sigler, who had been the chief executive officer of Champion International since 1974, had been sweating out a takeover, too, and had tried to generate enough cash to fend off the attack. But in 1984, Champion itself had bought St. Regis Corporation, acting as a so-called white knight after some other raiders had threatened to take over St. Regis.

As for the company itself:

Champion had operations in the United States, Canada, and Brazil. It manufactured paper for printing and for writing, as well as newsprint, publication paper, kraft, pulp, and forest products of all kinds. It also made paperboard for construction, and plywood, lumber, studs, pulp products of all kinds, and packaging products.

The company, in spite of its extensive holdings and its diversified production line, always appeared to be down in its stock price. In the late eighties it was trading just about where it had traded a decade before. And Buffett knew that the price was well under the actual book value of the company.

There were many reasons for Champion's low earning record. First, a worldwide situation had depressed conditions in the wood-products industry. The world pulp markets were weak. Prices on the company's lower paper grades had been forced down. There were financial difficulties in connection with several new subsidiaries. There was an increase in the corporate tax rate—most of that due to the company's business in Brazil, where political reforms had seriously impaired many once viable commercial enterprises.

In 1989 the company was producing about 1.4 million tons of coated and uncoated paper stock at four giant mills: in Canton, North Carolina; Courtland, Alabama; Hamilton, Ohio; and Pensacola, Florida.

Champion International had long bragged that one out of every three paperboard milk containers in the United States was made from Champion paperboard. It also had a huge building-products business, which was badly hurt by an extensive housing slump in the United States.

The company was simply unable to achieve a good profit profile from its undertakings, and was trading at a price/earnings ratio of about 7 times earnings.

On the minus side, the company had earned a reputation for being unable to make decent capital investments. Many of its capital investments had paid off badly, or lost money for the company.

On the plus side, the company still owned a tremendous amount of timberland: 6.4 million acres in the United States and 2.5 million in Canada. In Canada, Champion owned about 85 percent of Weldwood, a pulp and paper products company.

It was the 9 million acres of land covered with forest that intrigued other companies They all wanted part of it. That was where the money could be made.

Champion International employed about thirty thousand workers. In the past few years, before 1989, it had completed the biggest part of a huge modernization program started by management to keep the company in competition. Over $2 billion had been spent on capital projects, including the modernization program.

Warren Buffett had been a white knight in the attempted takeover of USAir, a company that was ripe for the right kind of attack. And he had served the purpose of a white knight in dealing with Gillette, although no one had made an out-and-out move on the company. He had improved the cash holdings to a point where Gillette could simply smile in the face of a threat.

Now Andrew C. Sigler got in touch with Warren Buffett and Buffett studied the papers on Champion International. He could see immediately that its stock was selling at a very low price, based on the value of the company's holdings.

When the deal was made, Buffett put in $300 million. Sigler had this to say:

"We wanted to raise capital to help support our cost-cutting, quality improvement, and capacity enhancement programs. Berkshire's CEO, Warren Buffett, is a remarkably astute investor, and his commitment to the long-term performance of the companies in which he invests is well matched to Champion's needs and goals.

"This infusion of capital from such a stable source is particularly valuable for a capital-intensive company such as ours during this period of economic uncertainty. It improves our balance sheet and strengthens our capability to complete our announced capital improvement program."

Buffett's deal was a profitable one for him as well. The preferred stock he bought guaranteed him 9 percent a year, along with an option to convert to common stock if the shares should rise—a "lottery ticket," in the words of Buffett biographer Roger Lowenstein. No matter what happened, that 9 percent would keep rolling in year after year as long as Buffett held the stock.

By no means did Warren Buffett's interest in investment stop with the three large deals he made in 1989. A follow-up project took place in 1990, and another in 1991. The 1990 deal had to do with Wells Fargo, and the 1991 deal had to do with American Express; both of these were solid companies faced with sudden downturns in business through no fault of their own.

Anyway, the investment world was startled once again on October 24, 1990, to learn that Warren Buffett had just purchased 5 million shares of Wells Fargo & Company, the California bank that had started out as a bank and delivery service just about a century and a half before. These 5 million shares represented almost 10 percent of the company's common stock.

Overnight Buffett had become the company's largest stockholder.

Wells Fargo was the brainchild of two men who had followed their fortunes to California to cash in on the

Gold Rush of 1848. They founded the company in 1852. Two years previous to the birth of Wells Fargo & Company, Henry Wells and William G. Fargo had founded another important company that was to be a long-lived company name—one called American Express.

The early days of Wells Fargo were dedicated mostly to the safe delivery of gold, silver, and money from the mines that were springing up everywhere in Northern California after the Sutter's Mill findings in 1848. Wells and his partner Fargo decided to blend two services— that of safe delivery of cash and that of safe banking of cash.

The idea was for the miners to deposit their gold dust and/or money with Wells Fargo, and let Wells Fargo either carry the money to its own bank or deposit it in another bank for the customer.

Holdups were frequent in the West, which was still wild and woolly, so the company armed its drivers and developed other safety measures to protect its bank branches from robbery. Making the delivery of money and gold safe in those days was an achievement that contributed to the development of the West Coast.

In its heyday, Wells Fargo transported not only by stagecoach, but by rail as well. It carried gold, it carried cash, it carried silver, and it carried passengers and baggage as well throughout the rugged terrain of the Western United States, Canada, and Mexico.

People grew to trust Wells Fargo. In 1905, the company broke up its two functions— banking and delivery— and the bank segment began to acquire other, less well-run banks throughout the far West.

Warren Buffett had experimented with Wells Fargo stock, buying about 30,000 shares of it for Berkshire Hathaway in 1989. The stock had always held up; the company was run well. But late in the eighties and early in the nineties, the banking business came under a cloud.

The savings and loan fiasco gave the very word "banking" a bad rap. In fact, generally speaking, banking at that time meant excess badmouthing by the investment fraternity, slashing of dividends, thousands of real estate loan writeoffs, and layoffs throughout the banking industry.

Those times, of course, were exactly *right* for Warren Buffett. He knew the company. He knew the reports. He had read the history a long time ago. The word on the Street was, "Wells Fargo's a dead duck"—that statement was uttered by a money manager and duly quoted in the *Wall Street Journal.*

Buffett didn't think so. He bought what he could get of Wells Fargo. The estimate was that he spent about $225 million, but it turned out that the real cost was closer to $289 million. That amount didn't matter at all to him. The stock, which kept waffling through 1991, soon steadied up, and began to rise.

In the end, when all the counting was done, it turned out that Warren Buffett had once again foiled the doubters and eventually *doubled* the money he had put into Wells Fargo, with the stock, purchased at about $58 a share, trading at around $150.

The next big Buffett buy was the American Express deal. On August 1, 1991, Buffett purchased about $300 million worth of their stock for Berkshire Hathaway.

The company, as has been mentioned, was founded in 1850 by the same Mr. Wells and Mr. Fargo who had brought Wells Fargo & Co. through its first years. In the 1990s, of course, American Express's main product was its credit card line, along with its traveler's checks, which seemed to be going out of fashion just a bit in favor of credit-card shopping on a global basis.

But the company also operated a financial planning department and involved itself in securities brokerage, asset management, international banking, and investment banking. In addition to the operations already mentioned, American Express owned Omaha-based American Express Information Services Corporation as well.

What precipitated the agreement between American Express and Berkshire Hathaway were a number of problems that had suddenly descended on American Express in 1989 and the early 1990s.

There was a money problem with Shearson Lehman, owned by American Express, that called for the parent company to pump more than $1 billion into the firm in 1990 to restructure it completely. American Express was still suffering from that outflow of cash.

The year before, in 1989, the company had been hit with a $30 million loss when it had trouble with another unit, the Boston Company, which specialized in lending money to wealthy individuals.

There were also loans to Prime Computer and Balcor Company, described as "worrisome," or "troublesome" by some money managers.

And the credit card segment itself came in for some carping criticism because many customers complained that AmEx was taking too large a commission for sales billed to its cards. This problem was more tricky than usual because of the intense competition running all through the credit-card industry. American Express was being undercut in its commissions and costs to an alarming degree.

So it was AmEx that came to Buffett this time, asking for an infusion of cash. Which, of course, Buffett was happy to provide.

The deal that was finally worked out provided Buffett with a dividend of 8.85 percent—something Warren Buffett referred to as a "perk," if indeed it was a perk.

The agreement between Berkshire Hathaway and American Express called for Buffett's nontransferable preferred shares to be exchanged for common stock within three or four years. American Express would redeem the securities issued to Berkshire by exchanging common shares for the preferred stock.

The financial pundits were mixed in their reactions to the deal. Allan Sloan, of *Newsweek*, wrote: "There's not much upside potential with this one. I'm not sure why he did it."

Buffett disagreed: "Convertible preferred shares have unlimited upside." But he did admit, "With this, we get less of an investment opportunity."

Buffett explained further to the *Wall Street Journal* why he had done it:

"When I heard they needed some equity funds, I told Jim [Robinson, chairman of American Express] that Berkshire would be interested in investing $500 million. I was willing to buy more, but Jim didn't want to sell more than $300 million."

And $300 million is what he invested.

At American Express, Buffett did not get a seat on the board, nor did he particularly want one. Did Buffett's strategy make him any money? A glance at the stock market reports shows that American Express, which was trading at about $25 at the time the deal was cut, was trading in the summer of 1997 at about $78.

CHAPTER FOURTEEN

Salomon Brothers: Investor

Warren Buffett had never attempted to hide his disdain for all the things that Wall Street stood for, particularly for him as an individual who had seen its workings close up. It was his distrust of Wall Street maneuvering that had caused him to return to his home base in Omaha, Nebraska, when he had finally had his fill of the Street's machinations.

One of his most quoted remarks had to do with his true feelings about the New York stock market:

"If a graduating MBA were to ask me, 'How do I get rich in a hurry?' I would not respond with quotations from Ben Franklin or Horatio Alger, but would, instead, hold my nose with one hand and point with the other toward Wall Street."

And yet on September 28, 1987, Buffett invested $700 million in preferred stock in Salomon Brothers, to the shock of almost everyone who had ever heard of Warren Buffett.

The fact that he had selected Salomon Brothers for his sudden plunge into market activity was even more of a surprise than the fact that he had decided to get his feet wet in the first place. For Salomon was the epitome of all that Warren Buffett disliked about Wall Street.

It was Buffett's one unbreakable law: Don't get involved in short-term trades or with those who do short-term trading. Yet here he was, savoring the moment, and at his next meeting telling stockholders, somewhat apologetically, somewhat hesitantly, what he had done, if not exactly why he had done it.

Nor did he present a rebuttal to the argument that he had violated all his lifelong credos in going along the route he had just chosen. Instead he would even admit, four years later, in the 1991 Berkshire annual report:

"We believe that according the name 'investor' to institutions that trade actively is like calling someone who repeatedly engages in one-night stands a romantic."

Unbelievably, there he was, standing up with a smile on his face, telling a *Wall Street Journal* reporter, "I like the fact it's a big transaction. I can't be involved in fifty or seventy-five things. That's a Noah's Ark way of investing—you end up with a zoo that way. I like to put meaningful amounts of money in a few things."

But, in the long run, he did admit something ruefully: "Without borrowing, it pretty much empties the piggy bank for now." In other words, for all intents and purposes, Buffett was tapped out.

Fact: Warren Buffett had deliberately and artfully gone against all his own precepts in plopping $700 million of his money into Salomon's lap. In fact, he was still temporizing about his move at the 1991 annual meeting.

"Why are we vocal critics of the investment banking business when we have a $700 million investment in Salomon? I guess atonement is probably the answer."

That, according to Buffett, was the reason he had decided to put all that money in a firm that was known throughout the industry for its razor-edged trading and its hair-trigger decisions: to atone for his lifelong antipathy to Wall Street and its inhabitants.

What Buffett did not know at the time he made his move, of course, was that within three weeks of that enormous investment, the stock market crash of 1987 would take place. On one day, the Dow average would drop 508 points, about 23 percent of the whole—making that day its worst single-day loss ever, worse even than Black Thursday in 1929.

Before the 1987 crash, Salomon's common stock was rated at about $32 a share; after the crash, common sank to $16 a share. It was a horrendous slide down a slippery slope.

But then, Warren Buffett had always looked out for the safety factor in any stock deal. He had *not* purchased common stock. He had purchased *preferred*. And therein lay the vast difference in the woes of those around him and those stockholders with him via Berkshire Hathaway.

Common stock represented a person's ownership in a company. With a rise in stock prices, an owner could make a very good profit if he sold at a higher price than he bought at. However, if the economy turned sour, and the stock went down, the owner of the stock lost.

Preferred stock was a very different animal. Preferred stock paid dividends to the owners of the stock *before* the dividends went to the holders of common stock. And, if the company folded, a preferred stockholder could claim the assets before the common stockholder could.

No matter what happened to the stock market, and as long as Salomon continued to pay dividends, Berkshire—and Warren Buffett—would not be affected by a drop in stock price. And so Salomon's 9 percent dividend—$63 million a year—would be paid to Berkshire, exempt from corporate taxes. (Corporations did not have to pay taxes on 70 percent of their dividend income on preferred stocks.)

That was the reason Buffett could quite frankly compare the investment game with a game of poker.

"If you're in a poker game and in the first half hour you don't know who the patsy is, *you're the patsy.*"

By that, Buffett meant the following:

"If the market goes down 10 percent and that upsets you, that means you think the market knows more about your business than you do. In that case, you're the patsy. If it goes down 10 percent and you want to buy more, because the business is worth just as much, *they're* the patsy."

Discussing the 1987 stock market crash with Adam Smith in *Esquire*, he said:

"Anything can happen in stock markets. That doesn't have to concern the investor. To the extent that silly instruments cause silly prices, he can take advantage of them. The rest of the time he can ignore them. If I'm a farmer in Washington County, and the farm next door is selling at a silly price, I don't say that's a terrible event. If I have the money, I buy it; if I don't, I watch somebody else buy it. I don't go out and buy six newsletters to find out what's going to happen to my farm."

The truth of the matter was that it was Salomon that had come to Warren Buffett at this time. Salomon had been badly caught in a downturn. The person who made contact with Buffett was John Gutfreund (pronounced "Good Friend"). He had become head of Salomon after Salomon was sold to Philbro Corporation; for a while he and David Tendler, of Philbro, had served as joint chairmen of the board. Then Gutfreund ousted Tendler and took over as head.

The company prospered in the underwriting business and was soon called "King of Wall Street" by *Business Week*. Things went along swimmingly until the crash of 1987. That was when the bond market collapsed—and

Gutfreund discovered that he was working with a tremendously bloated staff.

He had begun firing people to cut out the fat, but the results did not help the company any. The vultures were circling, sensing trouble at the fabled Salomon spread. Ronald Perelman, the well-known chairman of Revlon, had joined forces with junk-bond king Michael Milken in an effort to buy out the company.

Perelman's weapon for takeover was a 14 percent stake in Salomon controlled by Minerals and Resources Corporation of Bermuda. Minerals was owned by the Oppenheimer family of South Africa. It was a dangerous game at the climax, the confrontation of Gutfreund against Perelman and Milken, but when Gutfreund finally got Warren Buffett to come in with Berkshire's $700 million, Perelman turned to other, less astute prey.

There was a sense of desperation in Gutfreund's deal with Buffett. He had a difficult time ramming the deal through his own board of directors. Everybody inside knew what a favorable cut Berkshire was getting on the deal, and how unfavorable Salomon's cut was. Still, there was little else to be done with the obvious and hovering presence of Perelman, and the shadowy Milken in the background, making the game one of forlorn hope.

In the end, with the board members still obstinate, Gutfreund said that if the Buffett deal was rejected and the Perelman plan was adopted—thus giving the company over to Perelman—he would resign.

"I never stated it as a threat," Gutfreund said later. "I was stating a fact."

What made the deal with Buffett—or any deal for that matter—a problem was the melodrama that then surrounded activities at the usually placid Salomon enclave. Already there were murmurs of improprieties in trading, but as yet nothing too murky had been detected and articulated.

Mostly the company had flown pretty close to the wind in a number of lucrative oil dealings. And it had been fined a number of times for cheating customers both in securities and in commodities trades. In other words, the company did have a rather extensive history of underhanded transactions.

In addition, there was Gutfreund's lifestyle, which could generously be termed "life on the edge." He had always been a highflyer, open-handed with his money. He had always lived life to the hilt.

The tabloids and magazines soon began picking up on Gutfreund's shenanigans. He and his wife, who was a well-known New York socialite, bought an expensive duplex on Fifth Avenue. Magazine articles began hinting that the pair had spent a good $20 million "tidying up" their posh apartment. That $20 million was more than three times the original cost of the duplex. They also bought an apartment in Paris at no little expense. It was obvious they knew how to play the "beautiful people" game.

Gutfreund began to lay plans to extract a bit more money from the company for his own personal use. What he proposed seemed to be a simple bonus for his associates. But the plan was one of epic proportions: $120 million in bonuses to all the top Salomon brass! It was a ludicrous display in the midst of the company's desperate attempts to keep things afloat in a time of serious economic downturn.

When Warren Buffett heard this news he blew his top. This occurred in October 1990, three years after Buffett had saved Salomon's bacon. Buffett pleaded with Gutfreund to reduce the bonus figures substantially. Gutfreund paid no attention, and came up with another plan that *added* $7 million to the original staggering amount.

Buffett and Munger, who were serving on the board

after the Berkshire investment, voted no to Gutfreund's bonus plan, but the appropriation passed anyway.

The overspending went right on. For some time there had been an ambitious scheme to invest in and occupy a huge new office tower at New York City's Columbus Circle. The plan had already progressed to the point where a binder of $200 million was in the hands of the builders.

It was scrapped, with a forfeit of $100 million.

Instead, the company moved from One New York Plaza to nineteen floors at Seven World Trade Center nearby.

While Buffett did not spend all his time at Salomon, he attended board meetings and tried to keep things in a state of harmony, though it was hard with the flamboyant Gutfreund running things. Yet Buffett continued to throw business Salomon's way, and Salomon responded in kind.

Some of Berkshire's notes were underwritten by Salomon. And Salomon and Berkshire traded huge amounts of securities back and forth.

Quoting from Salomon's 1990 proxy statement:

"Among the company's transactions, in the ordinary course of its business in 1989, Salomon Brothers Inc. purchased from Berkshire entities in which it is informed Berkshire has a material interest, marketable securities having a value of approximately $884,663,000. Additionally, Berkshire paid commissions and fees of $3,086,000 to Salomon Brothers Inc. in connection with securities transactions. The company believes that its transactions with Berkshire and such entities are upon terms which are not less favorable to the company than those obtainable from other sources."

Meanwhile, Salomon traders were doing quite well. It was said that at least 106 of its executives had each made at least a million dollars. One had made $23 million.

Things were beginning to straighten out when suddenly everything took the opposite turn and began to fall apart again. It was the fault of a single person at Salomon. That is, the initial step was taken by one man, but the eventual flap, one of monumental proportions, was caused by the actions—or, more accurately, the total inaction—of a group of individuals.

A young new player at the game, Paul Mozer, was at thirty-four years of age in a position of considerable trust at Salomon. After joining the company as a bond salesman in 1979, he had worked his way up the ladder until the year 1988, when, after a two-year stint with John Meriwether, Salomon's best bond trader, he took over the government desk.

In that job Mozer attended U.S. Treasury auctions to make bids for the bonds the government issued regularly. Treasury securities were the world's biggest market, with $100 billion in daily trading. The bond dealers from Wall Street were a select few firms chosen by the Federal Reserve Bank of New York to trade the bonds.

Only these so-called primary bidders were allowed to submit bids on behalf of clients. There were thirty-nine primary dealers, of which Salomon was the oldest and the one with the biggest share of bonds.

These firms' traders were in continual contact by telephone with their peers at the Federal Reserve. It was only at the auctions that they confronted one another—the Feds to get the most money, the traders to get the best and lowest numbers. The auctions themselves involved "runners," whom the dealers stationed by the phones in the building. Just before a one o'clock deadline, the runners got their orders and wrote them out by hand, then dropped the bids into an old wooden box. And at one, the slot was closed.

It was all a little crazy, like something out of a silent movie. But the system had worked since its inception, when the U.S. government had begun financing its debts after World War I. At one time a J. P. Morgan trader had bid for half of an auction of T-bills. An attempt to corner the market? Perhaps. A new rule was instituted. No dealer could bid for more than 35 percent on each bond issue.

It was Paul Mozer who spotted a loophole. It was the *awards* that were limited to 35 percent, not the *bids*. In June 1990, acting on impulse, Mozer bid for double the total of notes on auction. Michael Basham, in charge of Treasury auctions, spotted the action, and warned him not to do it again.

But Mozer was a man who didn't bother too much about orders given to him. Two weeks later there was a $5 billion bond auction. He submitted a bid for $10 million. Basham then said that *bids* too would be limited to 35 percent. At this point Mozer began to go just a little berserk. He leaked the story to the press.

Treasury was stunned. Salomon tried to force Mozer to apologize, but it didn't quite come out that way. The company shipped him to London for a cooling-off period. What the company did not know was that in July and August Mozer had inflated his awards by bidding on behalf of customers who had not even authorized him to do so.

In February 1991 Mozer continued his machinations, in one case submitting phony bids on behalf of customers and submitting 35 percent bids for two customers as well as a genuine bid for Salomon.

An audit in April uncovered the truth. Mozer blamed it on the error of a clerk. Then in order to leave himself a loophole, he told Meriwether that he had submitted one false bid. Meriwether challenged him. Mozer lied again, swearing that was the *only* time.

On April 29 Meriwether met with Gutfreund; Thomas Strauss, Salomon's president; and Donald Feuerstein, general counsel, in the new headquarters at the World Trade Center.

Counsel felt Salomon should report the false bid, since it was probably criminal. But Gutfreund hesitated, thinking that it would probably all go away if nobody said anything. Gutfreund always believed in just a little bit of luck to help him out of tight spots.

Salomon refrained from acting without looking further into Mozer's fake bids. In May, Mozer made a high bid and was awarded $10.6 billion worth of bonds. He got 87 percent of the entire offering. The bonds were to be split among Salomon and two Salomon customers. But this time other dealers were unable to deliver notes that they could not get hold of because of Mozer's high-handed actions.

The price of two-year bids in May zoomed to the skies. Mozer made $18 million on what came to be called "the squeeze." He had also made $4 million earlier on his phony bids. This time the other dealers complained bitterly at having been burnt. Some were actually put out of business.

At Treasury, Basham saw what was happening and guessed who was in the driver's seat. He tipped off the Securities and Exchange Commission. SEC joined the Justice Department and began to look into Salomon's role in the squeeze.

In spite of what was brewing, Salomon was just beginning to look good after a few lean years. Gutfreund, who had a pretty good idea of what was going on, visited Robert Glauber, the Treasury undersecretary, in Washington. In spite of the fact that Gutfreund had guessed accurately the facts in the scam, he had reported none of it to Treasury. Instead, he defended the company's behavior and said he would be glad to help if he could.

In late June, Gutfreund discovered that Salomon was on the receiving end of a civil and criminal probe. He hired the law firm of Wachtell, Lipton, Rosen & Katz to investigate Salomon's behavior in the squeeze. And he never told Wachtell, Lipton about Mozer's false bid.

Finally, when the law firm uncovered hard evidence of false reporting, Salomon admitted the truth. Six bidding violations had occurred. Marty Lipton, the firm's senior partner, advised Gutfreund that he should make disclosure. Gutfreund agreed that he should.

On August 8, Gutfreund told the board of directors the truth. They were appalled. Immediately they got on the phone to Warren Buffett. When he heard the news, Buffett didn't seem all that concerned.

Gutfreund and Strauss called their contact Gerald Corrigan at the New York Fed, outlining the law firm's findings and saying that they knew of at least one false bid. Gutfreund made similar calls to SEC chairman Richard Breeden and to Glauber.

On Friday came a press release from Salomon. The release was incomplete. It did not say that Gutfreund and Strauss had known the truth for months. It seemed to the staff that the press release had gotten everybody off the hook. But this sense of false security did not last long.

On Monday, August 12, the *Wall Street Journal* focused on the roles of Gutfreund and Strauss. The wording gave the impression that Gutfreund was in on the bidding, which was untrue. But Gutfreund knew that in the future the focus of the story would be directly on him as CEO.

He called in Deryck Maughan, head of Salomon's investment bankers division, and William McIntosh, who ran the weekly sales meeting. He ordered Maughan and McIntosh to assure the members of Salomon that the problem had been solved. They obeyed his orders. The troops now thought that there would be no more trouble.

Of course, the problem was far from solved. Salomon's stock opened lower. And players who worked the short-term IOUs—its commercial paper—began to desert

Salomon. The marketplace was up to its neck in rumors. And these were rumors that could sink Salomon.

McIntosh met with Gutfreund and Strauss again, and this time suggested that Gutfreund resign. Gutfreund said he wouldn't resign. But he agreed to write another press release.

McIntosh met with Maughan. The two of them felt that they had been double-crossed by their employers. Maughan was a British citizen, a man who had made Salomon's Tokyo office a major profit center. He was in New York to try to breathe new life into Salomon's corporate finance department. A graduate of the London School of Economics, Maughan was thought of as Gutfreund's eventual replacement.

The top men at Salomon met at Wachtell, Lipton that night. It was there that they drafted a second news release. And this time they pointed the finger at exactly who was to blame: Gutfreund and Mozer.

Gutfreund became the higher-up in the know who had not reported wrongdoing by a subordinate. And that was to be his role as seen in the wide-ranging investigation that was now progressing.

Thursday was panic time at Salomon. Various agencies were cutting themselves off from the company. Gutfreund had become a pariah. Salomon's stock was in the process of dropping from 37 to 27. Everything was unraveling.

Friday morning Gutfreund's picture was right there at the top of the *New York Times*'s front page. It was the same thing as looking at his obituary. He phoned Corrigan at Treasury, and told him that he would be resigning from Salomon. Corrigan did not discourage him a bit. Lipton was the only one around who told him to hang in there.

But Gutfreund knew when his time was up.

He rang up Warren Buffett in Omaha. He told him

immediately that he had decided to quit because of the scandal that was developing all around him. He had called, he told Buffett, because he wanted Buffett's help.

What kind of help?

He wanted Buffett to take over the operation of Salomon Brothers.

Buffett was gun-shy. He hedged.

"You've got to come to New York," Gutfreund said. "I just read my obituary. Look at the paper."

Buffett already had. He said slowly, "Let me think about it."

CHAPTER FIFTEEN

Salomon Brothers: Savior

Warren Buffett faced the troops for the first time at a meeting in the Salomon auditorium. His audience was composed of managers of the firm. Gutfreund opened the meeting. He did not go in for any sad farewells, nor did he oblige with any ornate fanfare for Buffett. He said very quietly that Salomon was lucky to have a man like Buffett to take over in the present situation.

It was a meager adieu both for him and for Strauss.

At the podium, Warren Buffett started out establishing a stance on high moral grounds and promising only hard work and no rest until the company that had once been great would be great again. The main theme of his discourse was that Salomon would have to be much more circumspect than it had ever been before.

Buffett turned to tennis metaphors.

"I don't want anybody playing close to the line," he said. "Anything not only on the line, but near the line, will be called out." After all, he went on, "You can do very well hitting down the middle of the court."

No playing close to the line: That would be the order of the day as long as he was in control.

He went on to elaborate, but it was obvious what he meant—and that he meant what he said. Anyone not following his concept carefully and flat out would be in deep trouble.

Apparently his introductory talk served its purpose, for at the end of it, those in attendance burst into spontaneous applause for this man who would be their chairman for the crucial rebuilding period that was coming up.

The rest of the country, including much of Wall Street, was staring at the headlines that read "Salomon Says Buffett to Become Interim Chairman" and wondering, Who is this guy? In fact, *Barron's* did its usual tongue-in-cheek treatment of the story with the following lead by Alan Abelson:

"The caretaker appointed to look after Salomon in the absence of Gutfreund and Strauss is an out-of-towner, from Omaha, Nebraska, to be exact, and he runs a textile company. But he's supposed to be a fast learner, so we've no doubt he'll pick up enough about the securities business while on the job to keep the traders from sneaking off to play paddle ball or catch the 3 P.M. showing of *Terminator 2*."

Very amusing. The picture that emerged was one of a country hick seated at an old-fashioned loom, running up textured fabrics of one kind or another. The sobriquet "out-of-towner" certainly set the tone of sarcasm. A typical New York attitude. And it was a common one that day on the Street.

On Saturday morning, Buffett met with a dozen or so of Salomon's top brass for an informal but official get-together. It was to Buffett's advantage that he was the only one who knew how he was going to do what he would do. The rest of them had no inkling—in fact, some of them had never met him or even heard of him.

He took over the reins immediately in his quiet but forceful way. He looked at the executives and made his announcement. It was to the effect that he was going to select one of them right there in that room to become the manager of Salomon during the "reconstruction" period.

But first he was going to interview each of these men separately and in depth. "I'm going to meet with you one at a time," he said. "I'll ask you all the same question: 'Who should run this firm?' Come in any order you like."

With that, he left the room and shut the door. The interviews, brief but intense, followed. In the end, Buffett never said who was going to be the leader for the interim period that was to follow. Instead he opened up another meeting to get the full facts of the Salomon situation in his head. He knew only a few of the more obvious details.

A press conference was scheduled for Sunday afternoon, just after a long board meeting at which a number of issues would be discussed. However, the press conference became a much more spectacular event than was originally intended.

Even as Buffett and the top brass were scrambling through a crowd of media personnel jamming the entrance to 7 World Trade Center, the news came across to them by word of mouth: The Treasury Department had banned Salomon from its bond auctions.

This was grave news indeed. Salomon had been the leader of the pack for so long it would be unseemly for it not to be allowed to bid. And yet that was the edict, made public now by Treasury. No wonder the media had descended in such force—to watch the car wreck finally happen.

The board meeting itself was not without drama. First, and most important, the board accepted the resignations of John Gutfreund, Thomas Strauss, and John Meriwether. It then did what should have been done long ago in the past: it fired Paul Mozer as well as Thomas Murphy, Chairman of Capital Cities/ABC. Then it appealed to Secretary of the Treasury Nicholas Brady to lift, at least par-tially, the government's suspension of Salomon trading at auctions of Treasury securities.

During the board meeting Buffett had a telephone call from Secretary Brady. Buffett ticked off the actions that had already been taken in the board meeting. In addition, he told Brady how he would institute new procedures to prevent a recurrence of the false bidding.

Then Buffett put his own reputation on the line. He promised to clean house as thoroughly as he could. Later he said:

"I told him there were going to be controls that he could hold men responsible for in the future. . . . Similarly, that we were planning a future that would be considerably different than our past."

However, Buffett said, if Treasury was going to prevent Salomon from bidding at auctions, it would make no sense for him, Buffett, to continue as interim chairman. The call ended abruptly, with Brady saying he would get back to Buffett later.

When the board meeting broke up, Buffett sought out Deryck Maughan. He pulled him aside and said, "You're the guy." Maughan nodded. He knew what he was in for, but he was game.

The crowd of media types assembled at the press conference some minutes later, with all the usual noise and commotion associated with such get-togethers. Buffett finally came in and took over. He started off with a bang, introducing himself and Deryck Maughan as the two men in whose hands the fate of Salomon rested. But, he pointed out, he would be chairman—unsalaried, at that—for only as long as it took the company to climb up out of its myriad troubles.

And Buffett had good news, too. he had just received a phone call from Secretary Brady, he said, and Brady had agreed to allow Salomon to bid at Treasury auctions, but only for its own account, not for its customers. It was, as everybody knew, a limited reprieve—but at least a reprieve of sorts.

As the press conference progressed, Buffett became a lot more relaxed, and began to be more himself, with that easy wit flowing, and the answers coming a mile a minute. He used humor whenever he could, even in introducing himself. He would attempt to answer all reporters' questions, he said, "in the manner of a fellow that has never met a lawyer."

He started out by explaining that the illegal trading had first come to the attention of Salomon Brothers in April 1991, when Paul Mozer received a copy of a letter indicating the Treasury was aware of a problem in one of its auctions. And so on and so forth. Buffett's description of the details was hazy, but as accurate as he could get them at that point in time.

He said that Mozer had approached Meriwether and told him what had happened, because Mozer was sure he was going to be in deep trouble. Top management then discussed the matter with its lawyers, Buffett went on, and decided that it was mandatory that the government know what had been happening.

But, Buffett pointed out, it was not done.

"I cannot explain the subsequent failure to report," he said. He had always known and respected John Gutfreund, but this time he could not logically determine why the man had not taken the action he should have taken.

"The failure to report is, in my view, inexplicable and inexcusable."

Buffett promised to root out all the details of the scandal and then make changes that would improve the firm's reputation for honest bids.

Meanwhile, Buffett went to work at Salomon and kept a sharp eye on every detail there was to monitor. In a special note to shareholders, he wrote:

"An atmosphere encouraging exemplary behavior is probably even more important than rules, necessary though they are. During my tenure as chairman, I will consider myself the firm's chief compliance officer, and I have asked all nine thousand of Salomon's employees to assist me in that effort. I have also urged them to be guided by a test that goes beyond rules.

"Contemplating any business act, an employee should ask himself whether he would be willing to see it immediately described by an informed and critical reporter on the front page of his local paper, there to be read by his spouse, children, and friends. At Salomon, we simply want no part of any activities that pass legal tests but that we, as citizens, would find offensive."

The press was not uniformly pleasant to Buffett or to Salomon. The *Wall Street Journal* reported that Warren Buffett always stayed at the Plaza Hotel when he was in New York and that he wore expensive suits.

The truth of the matter was that Buffett usually stayed at Katharine Graham's apartment or at the Marriott near the World Trade Center. He used the Marriott so he could walk to work at Salomon. And he had few expensive suits, as anyone who knew him could attest.

But these were minor annoyances. Some of Salomon's business began to return—for example, the World Bank and the state of Massachusetts.

Buffett did make waves when he fired Salomon's lawyer, Donald Feuerstein. The furor arose mostly over who replaced him rather than the fact that he was let go. Buffett had selected Robert Denham to take the job. Denham was a managing partner the law firm of Munger, Tolles & Olson, a Los Angeles–based company founded by Charles Munger, Buffett's partner.

Denham had been a top student at Harvard Law School, and for seventeen year had worked with Buffett on Berkshire investments like American Express, Champion International, and even Salomon itself. But there were cries that Buffett was loading up the firm with close associates of his, rather than trying to choose replacements that would be best for the firm's future.

These carpings generally came to not much of anything. Buffett went on his own way in his inimitable manner. He began by confronting the sales force at Salomon, urging them to get in the game and work hard.

"It's my job to deal with the past," he told them. "It's your job to maximize the future, and it can be a huge future. Everyone must be his own compliance officer. That means that everything you do can be put on the front page of the newspaper, and there will be nothing that cannot stand up to scrutiny."

Warren Buffett knew that Salomon was being watched closely by the SEC, as well as the Treasury Department. He made it a point to visit Richard Breeden, chairman of the SEC, the agency that was investigating Salomon. Breeden said he had a reputation to uphold, and would dig into everything he could.

Buffett smiled. "Call us anytime someone doesn't give you what you want. You'll have a new person to deal with in twenty minutes."

It was said that Breeden was impressed. But that was Buffett's main claim to fame. He impressed the people he was dealing with—in exactly the way he wanted to impress them.

Now came the bad stuff.

With everyone outside looking in on Salomon and watching, Buffett had to make some very difficult changes. The main problem was the enormous bonuses that were always the rage around Salomon. He immediately caused most of the bonuses to be payable only in stock, and not in cash. This in turn reduced the debt. He also called for new procedures to cross-check every bid made at least twice. In the end the result looked good to those investigating Salomon.

If anyone had been worrying about Buffett's losing his focus on Berkshire Hathaway during his interim appointment at Salomon, that worry was resolved by Buffett himself.

"Berkshire works pretty well, some say, without me," Buffett noted. "It really is a lot less complicated operation than Salomon. I've always said I could run [Berkshire] working five hours a week. Maybe we'll test that. But I hope not for too long. . . .

"I was practically looking for a job. The only thing I am is an addressee on the envelope when they send me the check. . . . I can spent whatever time is needed. . . . If I quit thinking about this, I'd probably just have a big hope up there."

Soon Buffett's time was taken up by testimony before Congressional committees. On September 4, 1991, he testified before the House telecommunications and finance subcommittee. It was there that he apologized to the subcommittee.

"I would like to start by apologizing for the acts that have brought us here," he said. "The nation has a right to expect its rules and laws will be obeyed. At Salomon, certain of these were broken."

It was the apology itself that absolutely floored the subcommittee members. Had J. P. Morgan Sr. ever apologized? Absolutely not. He had been openly defiant of the government. Up to now almost all the captains of industry—and Wall Street—had refused to utter the dread "s" word, "sorry."

Buffett's vision of the "new Salomon" came across in these Buffettlike words:

"I want employees to ask themselves whether they are willing to have any contemplated act appear on the front page of their local paper the next day, to be read

by their spouses, children, and friends. . . . If they follow
this test, they need not fear my other message to them:
Lose money for the firm and I will be understanding; lose
a shred of reputation for the firm, and I will be ruthless."

At the end of the hearing, the chairman, Edward Mar-
key, asked Buffett to sum up his recommendations about
Salomon in one minute. Buffett's humor crept out even
then.

"I'm not sure I can drag it out for one minute. Integrity is paramount."

It was a fitting end to the testimony.

One week later he was in the hot seat again. But it
was a comfortable fit now, not a scorcher. On September
11, this is what he said:

"A week ago when I testified before the House subcommittee, I began by apologizing for the misdeeds of
Salomon employees that have brought us here. Normally
I would not wish to be repetitious. But in my opinion
this particular message bears repetition many times over.
The nation has a right to expect its rules and laws to be
obeyed, and Salomon did not live up to this obligation.

"Our customers have a right also to expect that their
names will not be drawn into some underhanded scheme.
So to you and them and the American people I apologize
on behalf of more than eight thousand honest and decent
Salomon employees as well as myself.

"Mr. Chairman, I also want to thank you for holding
these hearings in such a timely manner. You and the
American people have a right to know exactly what went
on at Salomon Brothers and I am here to tell you the full
truth as I know it to date. When and if I learn more, it
will immediately be disclosed to the proper authorities.

"Many decades ago J. P. Morgan stated the objective
of his firm: 'First-class business run in a first-class way.'
I have yet to hear of a better goal. It will guide me at

Salomon Brothers and I invite you to measure our future conduct by that yardstick."

The results of the third quarter of 1991 at Salomon were much better than anyone had expected. In fact, even with the $200 million that had been set aside to cover expected costs and fines, the firm made $85 million profit for the quarter. Buffett's revamping of Salomon's pay system cut the payroll by about $110 million.

To spread the good news, Buffett took out a two-page ad in the *Wall Street Journal*, the *New York Times*, and the *Washington Post* at a cost of about $600,000. It was in the form of a letter to shareholders about the company's shrunken balance sheet.

The letter, headlined "Salomon Inc., a Report by the Chairman on the Company's Standing and Outlook," detailed Buffett's survey of the situation and then listed his objectives in solving the company's problems. The business of setting aside money for potential fines was explored, along with Buffett's decision to cut back the bloated bonuses certain employees were getting, and the basic problem of rectitude and integrity of Salomon employees. The company's balance sheet was included in the ad, along with a repeat of J. P. Morgan's quotation on "first-class business" operation. The letter was typical of Warren Buffett's clear-headed expository style and was a masterpiece of public relations communication.

"I believe that we had an extremely serious problem, but not a pervasive one," Buffett said in response to a question about it. He had convinced many doubters.

Malcolm S. Forbes Jr. made the definitive statement about Buffett's chairmanship of Salomon in those crucial days: "I believe Salomon would have gone under without Warren Buffett. There was no question he saved it."

Buffett spent $290 million in getting Salomon out of the deep trouble in which the firm was mired. But it was a small price to pay for keeping the firm from being caught up in numerous criminal charges. These charges could easily have sunk the company forever.

He was quite sanguine about what he had accomplished:

"We have managed to preserve a firm with a proud history and promising future." He had used his own personal qualities—honesty, openness, caution, and fair-mindedness—to bring about a corporate change at Salomon Brothers that put the company where it should be rather that where it had found itself after a confidence-shaking crisis had skewed its image.

When Buffett had finished his interim chairmanship there was a great deal of speculation as to whom he would select to fill his shoes when he left. In the end Buffett chose Robert Denham to take over as chief executive officer.

CHAPTER SIXTEEN

The Baby Berkshires

Offhand, the sudden emergence in 1996 of the "Baby Berkshires" might have seemed an inspiration from the fertile brain of Warren Buffett—something created in order to launch a new stock named after Berkshire Hathaway, the highest-rated stock in existence and the most successful investment tool ever crafted by an individual investor.

That is, the naive might have thought, with Berkshire Hathaway stock trading at the unheard-of price of around $33,000 a share at the time, that Warren Buffett was trying to get quick cash in order to finance some humungous deal of his own. But the naive would have been absolutely wrong.

What started the cleverly named Baby Berkshires was an idea in the mind of Michael Ford, a man not known for being close to anyone at all on Wall Street. Ford was a political consultant who had worked for the liberal Democrats. And he was a lucky man in his Wall Street deals—he had already bought three Berkshire Hathaway shares, and was ecstatically happy with them.

With an investment idea in his head, but unable to

bring it to fruition, Ford ran into a promoter named Samuel Katz, a Philadelphia man who was in the business of financing sports arenas. In a casual conversation, Katz learned about Ford's three shares of Berkshires and oohed and aahed over them enough to flatter Ford a bit. Ford admitted that he was lucky: the shares had escalated in value to an unbelievable degree.

It was too bad, Katz lamented, that more people couldn't afford to buy Berkshires. But of course, the difficulty of purchasing the stock was the fact that the shares cost so much; it kept the stock in the hands of very few people, most of them incredibly rich already—or those well on their way there. Nobody else could really count on getting them.

As Ford and Katz talked, however, Ford admitted that he had an idea for a grand investment venture. But he didn't know how to bring it off. He thought there might be a way to reduce the cost of the Berkshire stock and get it into the range of the average lower-middle-class investor. The modus operandi would be to split up the stock into smaller units and reissue them in small hunks.

In other words, Ford and Katz would purchase a regular Berkshire, and break it up into maybe two dozen slices, and resell each of the slices. It would be similar to what happened when a stock was split by the issuing company into two shares for one.

To accomplish this job of splitting up Berkshires, Ford and Katz came up with a vehicle called the Affordable Access Trust. The scheme went this way: The Trust would purchase Berkshire shares, split them into multiple parts, and sell the smaller bits to less affluent investors. The Trust would make its money by charging a fee for the resale. It would use its profits to buy new Berkshire shares to be broken up and resold.

Ford wrote up the idea of the Affordable Access Trust and its issues and sent it in letter form to Warren Buffett.

Buffett promptly went through the roof. To put it mildly, he did not like the idea of someone else making money on his talents. He had made Berkshire Hathaway what it was by being an astute investor—probably the most astute of the century. He also felt that the pair marketing slices of Berkshires would be gouging small investors. Not only that, the action would hurt the good name that Buffett had built up for Berkshire Hathaway through the years.

In addition, Buffett could see that the Affordable Access Trust's purchase of Berkshire shares might artificially inflate the price of Berkshire stock, thus overpricing what Buffett had always claimed was underpriced.

There was no real way for Warren Buffett to prevent these two mavericks in the Street from doing what they wanted to do, and so Buffett and Munger got their heads together to try to figure out some way to stymie the operators or head them off at the pass, as it were.

The Affordable Access Trust went right on ahead, asking to register $250 million worth of units with the SEC, although both Ford and Katz thought that $35 million worth would be a more likely figure to shoot for. The Trust knew the difficulties, too. A Berkshire Hathaway was a hard share to buy. There were only 1.19 million shares, almost half of these owned by Buffett. And the rest were owned by hard-nosed long-termers who maintained a death grip on them, and had held on to them for years.

For example, in 1995, the trading volume for Berkshire Hathaway was less than 45,000 shares, around 175 a day. Nothing at all to speak of. A rarity, indeed.

Meanwhile, back at the Omaha Ranch. . . .

Buffett and Munger had to work fast. They had a vague idea of what they would do. Yet it would take the approval of the board in order to do it. And that meant hard work right away. The announcement came in the middle of February 1996.

Instead of trying to circumvent the Affordable Access Trust, or blocking it at the pass, Berkshire was in a sense *joining* Ford and Katz in their interesting ploy of marketing Berkshires at a low price. Or if not exactly joining them, Buffett at least was joining them in competing for public support.

For Berkshire's ploy was exactly the same as the Trust's. Berkshire would issue a brand-new stock called a Class B share of Berkshire Hathaway. The original Berkshire stock would be known as Class A stock. Each new Class B share would be exactly one-thirtieth of a Class A share. The Class A shares would still cost about $33,000— or whatever the shares were trading for at the time the Class B stocks were issued—and the Class B shares would be sold at about $1,000 a share.

When the idea was first released to the press, the most important thing about the news was the fact that Warren Buffett was at the same time offering a new stock on the market but playing down its worth and, in effect, telling people *not* to buy it! For example, in the 1996 annual report, he put it this way: "As I write this—with Berkshire stock at $36,000—I do not consider it undervalued." But he went on: "Berkshire is selling at a price at which . . . I would not consider buying it."

Allan Sloan wrote in *Newsweek*: "This makes Buffett the only corporate chairman I know to warn investors away from stock the company plans to sell. Such candor is an example of why Buffett is revered while other billionaires are treated as greedheads."

On May 6, 1996, Berkshire shareholders approved the plan of issuing the "Baby Berkshire" stock, although there was some opposition. Most shareholders were of the opinion that the Baby Berkshires would diminish the true value of the Class A shares.

Buffett disabused one individual who brought up the concern. "We wouldn't be doing this if we thought it would hurt present shareholders. We designed it so it wouldn't hurt present shareholders." He pointed out that the new shares were being offered to head off unit investment trusts—exactly like Affordable Access Trust planned to be—that would purchase Berkshire shares and resell them in bits and pieces. He warned investors that these trusts would charge large sales commissions and fees.

Shareholders were worried about Warren Buffett's newly acquired high profile in the investment business. "I don't think you have as good a handle as some of us do on the renown that you carry outside of Omaha, Nebraska," one shareholder said.

Buffett: "My first reaction is that maybe I should tell my barber that we should save the clippings and sell them."

Buffett assured them that the 350,000 shares of Baby Berkshires would attract people who wanted to buy and hold it instead of people who would want to buy and sell it the next day.

When the offering went on the market in May, investors sank $500 million into the Baby Berkshires—at least five times what Buffett had originally planned to sell.

In all, at least forty thousand new shareholders joined the ranks of Berkshire holders through the introduction of the Baby Berkshires. Warren then issued an "owner's manual" to welcome these new shareholders. In the folder, Buffett repeated his famed thirteen fundamental business principles (they are briefly noted at the end of this chapter), and he added new comments on investing.

He then reiterated his hope that Berkshire's stock would be valued honestly and fairly rather than over- or undervalued. For, he explained, fair value would make Berkshire stock very attractive to investors in for the long-term venture rather than those in for the short-term buy-and-sell-quick method.

Of course, it was impossible for him, Buffett, to control the price of the stock's shares, he went on. But it *was* within his power to invest in a rational and coolheaded manner rather than produce situations that might lead other investors to go in for the quick profit.

He actually preferred a stock market that was under-valued, rather than one heated-up and overvalued. He told his stockholders that if the market went down, they should not worry at all, since it was normal and only foretold a rise in the future. It would in fact, be good news for Berkshire.

There was more good news for Berkshire in the 1996 purchase of Capital Cities/ABC by the Walt Disney Company. And that merger was actually and more or less directly the result of a conversation inspired by Warren Buffett—a conversation between Tom Murphy, chief executive of Capital Cities, and Michael Eisner, the head of Disney.

It was a July day in 1995, as Buffett remembered it, when he was going to meet Murphy to play a round of golf. On the way to the clubhouse, he encountered Eisner. "We chatted briefly, and the subject of a possible combination of Disney and Cap Cities came up."

Eisner and Buffett waited for Murphy to arrive, which he did, in a few minutes. Then there was a short conversation that more or less centered on such a possible merger. Although there were no positive details dropped at the time, the attitudes on both sides of the fence—Eisner's and Murphy's—was that such a combination might indeed work out well.

Buffett has always been a little apologetic about the scene thus described. Actually, he noted to a reporter once, *he* had no motivation to get the other two men to-

gether. It just kind of happened. The fact is, the deal probably would have come up anyway in the future sometime.
Buffett's chance presence simply hurried things up.

The deal between Disney and Capital Cities was a
heavy one—one in the area of $20 billion. In the end, it
was Warren Buffett who acted as a kind of upper-class
bagman for the two big companies. In its own way, it
was a typically laid-back scene in a drama of powerful
men making big deals together.

Here's the action:

On March 5, 1996, Warren Buffett entered the Manhat-
tan offices of Harris Trust with two envelopes in his
pocket. At the bank, Buffett handed the two envelopes to
an officer of the firm.

Envelope Number 1 was stock worth $2.5 billion. It
was, in effect, Berkshire Hathaway's 20 million shares of
Capital Cities/ABC stock. It was being delivered to the
purchaser of that firm—the Walt Disney Company.

Envelope Number 2 contained . . . a secret. The outside of the envelope was marked: "Do not open until 4:30
P.M. on March 7." This was just a bit of showbiz invented
by Buffett himself. He wanted the sale of the company
kept secret even from the management of both Disney
and Capital Cities. And he also wanted it kept secret as to
how Berkshire would be paid for the contents of envelope
Number 1.

Buffett had the choice of taking a standard package—
Disney stock plus cash—or requesting all stock or all cash.

The secret remained just that, all parties playing the
game devised by Buffett, until March 7, when Buffett finally arrived to speak to Eisner late in the day. What had
happened in the meantime was a big plus for Eisner.

In effect, Buffett had given the best thumbs-up of all to
the deal, and to Disney in particular. Buffett had paid the
company and its boss the ultimate compliment by en-
trusting them with Berkshire's money. That is, he had

asked for stock only in Disney, rather than part cash or all
cash.

The 20 million Disney shares Buffett owned would
give Berkshire a minimum of a 3 percent stake in the new
Disney Company.

Buffett would have been paid $2.5 billion if he had
elected to receive his emolument in cash as part of Disney's $20 billion buyout of Cap Cities; he had bought
his Cap Cities stock for $345 million in 1986. Not a bad
investment—at least on paper!

And, in addition to the stock he already had in Disney, Buffett admitted that he had been buying up all the
Disney shares he could find on the market, adding to the
20 million he already had.

In Berkshire's 1995 annual report, Buffett acknowl-
edged that he was returning to the scene of an investment
crime, more or less. He had been attracted to Disney in
the first place by its extremely good film library. And in
addition, he'd liked Disney's growing theme-park business all over the globe. The low rates of Disney shares
also attracted him. The company was capitalized at less
than $90 million.

Way back, Buffett had invested a chunk of Buffett
Partnership money in the stock at the price of thirty-one
cents a share. The stock had just recently sold for $65 a
share. Buffett, in the meantime, had hung around for a
while, but had sold out in 1967 at the price of forty-eight
cents a share.

Buffett: "Oh, well. It's nice to be back."

In June 1996, Buffett rejoined the *Washington Post*'s
board of directors. He had been on the board in 1974, but
was forced to resign in 1986 when regulators told him he
couldn't also be on the board of Cap Cities. Disney's purchase of Cap Cities left him free to rejoin the *Post*. He
did so.

*   *   *

In December 1995, Warren Buffett had reported that Berkshire Hathaway doubled its investments in McDonald's Corporation during that year. Berkshire held 9.34 million McDonald's shares at the end of September 1995. They were worth $357.3 million. They were twice the 4.7 million McDonald's shares Berkshire held at the end of June 1995. Those were valued at $181.9 million.

Once news of the filing was released, the stock at McDonald's rose $1.75 to close at $48.13 on the New York Stock Exchange.

By the end of 1996, Berkshire owned 30.2 million shares of McDonald's, purchased at $41.96 a share. Berkshire had a 4.3 percent stake in the fast-food chain. The shares closed in March 1997 at $44.125.

Berkshire's ownership of McDonald's was up sharply from the 9.34 million shares held at the end of September 1995. The annual report did not comment on the additional holdings or the reason that Buffett had acquired them.

In his letter to shareholders, he was much more voluble about the stock market in general, warning investors that when the market was overheated, the investor was automatically paying more for the stock than it was really worth. And he reminded them that it frequently took a long time for the stocks to readjust and reflect their true value.

His letter went on to discuss his so-called buy-and-hold strategy for Berkshire Hathaway stocks. For example, the stakes were high on many very large companies.

- Berkshire owned more than 10 percent of American Express.
- It owned more than 10 percent of the Washington Post Company.
- It owned more than 8 percent of Coca-Cola.
- It owned more than 8 percent of Gillette.
- It owned more than 8 percent of Wells Fargo.

- It had a stake of 3 percent in Walt Disney after Disney's takeover of Capital Cities/ABC.
- It owned 4.3 percent of McDonald's.

After the issuance of the Baby Berkshire sin 1996, Warren Buffett had found himself discouraging investors from purchasing them. But forty thousand new investors were not discouraged. They bought anyway.

However, the price of the Baby Berkshires fluctuated a bit, then came back down to the original level. The movement of the Baby Berkshires caused the Class A Berkshires to gyrate a bit as well. With all the publicity Buffett got in warning people away from the Baby Berkshires, there was a carryover to the Class A Berkshires. The trading price had reached a peak of $38,800 just before the issuance of the Baby Berkshires. Now, with the discouragement of further investment in Berkshire, the Class A shares took a beating at first.

They dropped to as low as $30,000 some weeks later. They eventually began to recover, but never got back to their original peak height of $38,800. In March 1997, they were trading at $36,900.

Buffett: "The price, relative to value, is now more appropriate."

The Baby Berkshires were issued at the price of $1,100 each in May 1996, and from that time went up and then down. In March 1997, they closed at $1,233.

The success of the Baby Berkshires—issued, obviously, as a desperation move to curtail the profits of a competing company—caused pressure once again on Buffett to split Berkshire Hathaway stock in order to make it more affordable for the average investor.

Buffett continued to resist splitting. It was his reluctance from the beginning to split Berkshire that had made it the most expensive on a per-share basis of any stock in the country. However, the birth of the Baby Berkshires was essentially a split—into more than two pieces.

In spite of the cordial manner in which the public received his Baby Berkshires, Buffett was not entirely ecstatic over the acrobatic gyrations of the stock market at the end of 1996 and the beginning of 1997.

The truth was that Berkshire Hathaway's net worth had zoomed up 36 percent during the year—an advance not to be sneered at by anyone. And yet Warren more or less hinted in his 1997 annual report that the market was . . . well, uh . . . overheated?

Buffett: "Now, I didn't say *quite* that. But I said that there's always a danger in stocks getting ahead of the business, and I say that the risk of that seems fairly high now. That's not a market prediction, it's just a valuation judgment."

He was asked what a smart investor should be doing in a time when the market might appear overpriced.

Instead of answering the question, he told what *he* always did. "We look for good businesses run by good people and try and buy them at a sensible price, and that's pretty tough in the market now. But we'll keep working at it."

And he elaborated: "If you own good businesses, you stay with them. I mean, you don't try and jump in and out of the market. It's too tough. I mean, you may be wrong. And when you sell, you may not get another chance to buy intelligently. So if you own businesses that you really feel good about for five years or ten years, you just forget about it. The average investor would be better off if he bought a stock with the idea the market was going to be closed for five years."

But what about paying too much to buy a stock in that kind of market?

"I think the valuations *are* high and I said one time— a long time ago—that you pay a high price in the market for a cheery consensus. And you've got a pretty cheery consensus now. But . . . that's no reason to panic and it's not a market prediction."

He mentioned the joy of owning big chunks of successful businesses like Coca-Cola, Gillette, and American Express. "We stay with those. Those are wonderful businesses and we're fortunate to own big pieces of them and they're going to be worth a lot of money, in my opinion, ten or fifteen years from now and that's what we're all about."

The "thirteen principles" were Warren Buffett's attempt to outline his own broad scheme of operation to the people who had invested with him. The principles are paraphrased here in extremely brief form:

1. Buffett and Munger look upon their shareholders as partners rather than just investors in the usual sense.

2. They like their shareholders to have a major portion of their net worth invested in Berkshire Hathaway.

3. They judge Berkshire's performance on its intrinsic business value on a per-share basis, rather than by its size alone.

4. They prefer to own 100 percent of businesses rather than just pieces of them, although they admit this is not always possible.

5. They try to impart as much definite information as possible in their annual reports so that their investors can see how they are doing.

6. They try to clarify the actual workings of the stocks by regularly reporting "look-through" earnings,

excluding capital gains and purchase-accounting adjustments.

7. They insist on acting most conservatively in their borrowing policies, that is, they try to structure their loans on long-term fixed-rate bases.

8. They are interested only in acquiring companies that will raise the per-share intrinsic value of Berkshire's stock.

9. They try to check their "noble intentions" to hang on to stocks a long time to make sure their actions delivered shareholders $1 of market value for each $1 retained.

10. They do not issue common stock other than when they receive as much in business value as they give. (This held true even when the Baby Berkshires were issued.)

11. They hold to the theory that they have no intention of selling a business that Berkshire owns, no matter how much profit it might make.

12. They promise to be utterly candid in their reports to their shareholders, emphasizing the pluses and minuses of the year. "Candor benefited good managers."

13. They admit to discussing activities in marketable securities only to the extent legally required. Thus, there would be no talk about investment plans at all until the actions were already taken.

CHAPTER SEVENTEEN

Nine Keys to Investing

Warren Buffett would be the first person to admit that he never stumbled upon one specific "big secret" that made him the superb investor that he is. In fact, he never really knew how he was able to make his investments pay off as well as they did. Indeed, many of them did *not* come off well because he made mistakes just as anybody else would in putting his money on the wrong stock now and then.

It was simply the way Warren Buffett looked at life and lived it that made him what he eventually became—at one time, the richest man in the country.

He was strong in certain key elements of character and attitude; these were important factors in his success as an investor. A few of these elements should be examined more carefully by anyone wishing to follow in his footsteps. None are magical in any way. They are simply strengths that Buffett either trained himself to have, or that he had already and used naturally.

I. Know the Numbers and What They Mean

First and foremost, anyone who wants to be an investor must understand the fundamentals of mathematics. Numbers are the essence of the game. And that does not mean that there are a lot of Einstein-like formulas that can be used to make a fortune in the stock market; *there aren't any such things.*

The kind of arithmetic that is essential is a simple but accurate understanding of accounting, of profits and losses. It deals with specifics, and it is these specifics that determine exactly which investment will pay off and which will not.

Understanding numbers is essential in ascertaining the value of a company. But for the unwary, figures can be confusing. You must have full control of the figures in your mind or you may be easily fooled.

"When managers want to get across the facts of the business to you, it can be done within the rules of accounting," Buffett has said. "Unfortunately, when they want to play games, in at least some industries, it can also be done within the rules of accounting. If you can't recognize the differences, you shouldn't be in the equity-picking business."

The hopeful investor should have a grasp on the logic of moneymaking and the common sense of letting money grow for you.

"You don't need to be a rocket scientist," Buffett has warned. "Investing is not a game where the guy with the 160 I.Q. beats the guy with the 130 I.Q. Rationality is essential."

A bit of clear-headedness is needed as well.

"You're dealing with a lot of silly people in the marketplace; it's like a great big casino, and everyone else is boozing. If you can stick with Pepsi [these days he might say Coca-Cola], you should be okay."

"Casino" is the word to stress. Certainly, the market-place can be a gamble—a place where a person can lose his shirt. Or win a fortune. Watch out for the men and women who cut a wide swath through life and pay little attention to the rules of the game.

"The propensity to gamble is always increased by a large prize versus a small entry fee, no matter how poor the true odds may be. That's why Las Vegas casinos advertise big jackpots and why state lotteries headline big prizes."

In fact, Buffett shuns gamblers and gambling. Gambling can be the death of the market when it becomes a way of life—especially when a long surge of bull-market years blinds everyone to the fact that what goes up must eventually come down.

"We do not need more people gambling on the nonessential instruments identified with the stock market in the country, nor brokers who encourage them to do so. What we need are investors and advisers who look at the long-term prospects for an enterprise and invest accordingly. We need the intelligent commitment of investment capital, not leveraged market wagers. The propensity to operate in the intelligent, prosocial sectors of capital markets is deterred, not enhanced, by an active and exciting casino operating in somewhat the same arena, utilizing somewhat similar language, and serviced by the same workforce."

Still, in spite of all the talk of big bucks and bull markets and so on, Warren Buffett still depends heavily on simple mathematical chores, not complex formulas of an esoteric nature.

"If calculus were required," he has said, "I'd have to go back to delivering papers. I've never seen any need for algebra. Essentially, you're trying to figure out the value of a business. It's true that you have to divide by the number of shares outstanding, so division is required.

"If you were going out to buy a farm or an apartment house or a dry-cleaning establishment, I really don't think you'd have to take someone along to do calculus. Whether you made the right purchase or not would depend on the future earning ability of that enterprise, and then relating that to the price you are being asked for the asset." And once the simple arithmetic is done, there's no more need to use figures.

II. Invest in Products You Understand

The next most important element of Warren Buffett's method of operation is perhaps the most obvious. In fact, he has said time and time again exactly what he does when he looks for something to invest in. He looks for something he can *understand* himself.

For example, Berkshire had purchased 4 million shares of General Foods Corporation. Then in October 1985 it made a profit of $332 million when Philip Morris Company bought the firm. General Foods owned familiar brand names of all kinds.

"I can understand Kool-Aid," Buffett said, underlining his interest in companies making things he could see and touch.

Buffett has pointed out that not confining Berkshire Hathaway to the purchase of a specific kind of stock has given the company a much better chance of buying up new firms that make things that are understandable, rather than esoteric stocks in companies that make technologically complicated products.

"We're not in the steel business [at Berkshire], per se. We're not in the shoe business, per se. We're not in any business, per se. We're big in insurance, but we're not committed to it. We don't have a mind-set that says you have to go down this road. So we can take capital and move it into businesses that make sense."

Nor did Buffett ever use the market for any kind of guideline to his investment policies.

"The market is there only as a reference point to see if anybody is offering to do anything foolish. When we invest in stocks, we invest in businesses."

And yet, investing in a business is not *running* a business. Buffett has noted:

"Could you really explain to a fish what it's like to walk on land? One day on land is worth a thousand years of talking about it, and one day running a business has exactly the same kind of value. Running a business really makes you feel down to your toes what it's like."

Buffett's advantage over other investors has tended to be the fact that he had a greater understanding of the companies than his competitors did. And he was quick to leap on the stock of a suddenly beleaguered company that he knew to be sound.

"Investing gives you this wide exposure that you just can't get directly. As an investor you learn where the surprises are—in retailing, for example, where business can just evaporate. And if you're a really good investor you go back and pick up fifty years of vicarious experience. You also learn capital allocation. Instead of putting water in just one bucket, you learn what other buckets have to offer."

The ability to read a company's profile immediately has always helped Buffett know which ones to invest in and which ones to shun.

"I'm like a basketball coach. I go out on the street and look for seven-footers. If some guy comes up to me and says, "I'm five-six, but you ought to see me handle the ball,' I'm not interested."

III. Read Widely to Value Prospects

The third factor that made Buffett a great investor was his ability to size up and assess almost instantly the actual value of a company. His innate common sense and his clarity of vision enabled him to see through artifices and exaggerations about a company's strengths and weaknesses.

And it led him to make many important and profitable decisions.

"If we find a company we like, the level of the market will not really impact our decisions. We will decide company by company. We spend essentially no time thinking about macroeconomic factors.

"In other words, if somebody handed us a prediction by the most revered intellectual on the subject, with figures for unemployment or interest rates, or whatever it might be for the next two years, we would not pay any attention to it.

"We simply try to focus on businesses that we think we understand and where we like the price and management. If we see anything that relates to what's going to happen in Congress, we don't even read it. We just don't think it's helpful to have a view on these matters."

One of Warren Buffett's maxims has been repeated many times:

"Price is what you pay. Value is what you get."

About stocks that are underpriced, he once had this to say:

"It doesn't have to be rock bottom to buy it. It has to be selling for less than you think the value of the business is, and it has to be run by honest and able people. But if you can buy into a business for less than it's worth today, and you're confident of the management, and you buy into a group of businesses like that, you're going to make money."

He has always been able to evaluate companies from afar because he does a tremendous amount of research on any one company before investing money in it. Someone once asked him how he could discover the true value of a business when he was not in the business itself.

"Do a lot of reading," Buffett advised his interrogator. And he went on to explain. "I read annual reports of the company I'm looking at and I read the annual reports of the competitors—that is the main source of material."

IV. Always Maintain a Margin of Safety

The fourth key element that made Warren Buffett a good investor was his innate caution. He was definitely not a man who ever knowingly took a risk of any kind. Every move he made he calculated in advance, especially for the factors that might cause him to lose any of his investment money.

To quote again his two most well-known business principles:

"Rule Number 1: Never lose money. Rule Number 2: Never forget Rule Number 1."

To elaborate on these principles, Buffett has time and again returned to the basic investment philosophy of his chief mentor, Ben Graham.

"I consider there to be three basic ideas," Buffett has observed, "ideas that if they are really ground into your intellectual framework, I don't see how you could help but do reasonably well in stocks. None of them are complicated. None of them take mathematical talent or anything of the sort. [Ben Graham] said you should look at stocks as small pieces of business. Look at [stock market] fluctuations as your friend rather than your enemy— profit from folly rather than participate in it."

And then Buffett went on to paraphrase Graham's advice in the last chapter of his book *The Intelligent Investor:*

"He said the three most important words of investing: 'margin of safety.' I think those ideas, one hundred years from now, will still be regarded as the three cornerstones of sound investing."

In order to make his advice as clear as possible, Buffett has elaborated many times on exactly what he means by the "margin of safety":

"I put heavy weight on certainty. . . . If you do that, the whole idea of a risk factor doesn't make any sense to me. You don't do it where you take a significant risk. But it's not risky to buy securities at a fraction of what they're worth."

Or, of course, you could always follow the advice of Will Rogers, whom Buffett loves to quote.

Rogers had two rules to follow in investment. He would study the market carefully before purchasing any stock. Then he would follow his Rule Number 1: "When the stock doubles, sell it."

But, he was asked, what if the stock didn't double?

Then he would follow Rule Number 2: "If it doesn't double, don't buy it."

V. Become a Fanatic about Investment

The fifth key element of Warren Buffett's character that helped make him the astute investor he became was his absolute faith in what he was doing and his ability to concentrate to the exclusion of everything else on the strengths and weaknesses of companies he wanted to invest in.

In other words, what made Buffett a great investor was the same thing that makes a concert pianist great—as in the old vaudeville saw:

MAN ON STREET CORNER: How do you get to Carnegie Hall?

MUSICIAN: Practice, practice, practice.

Investment must be one's ruling passion if one is to become a successful investor, and what helps a person become so obsessed is not greed, as Buffett has often noted, but the fun of seeing the money grow over the years. Buffett turned his own idea of dedication to the job into a make-believe employment form that, if he were hiring someone to be an investor, he would confine to one question and one question only.

"Are you a fanatic?"

The greatest of the great investors *are* fanatics, Buffett has declared time and again.

VI. Avoid Buying "Popular" Stocks

No one is more closemouthed than Warren Buffett about the stocks he is interested in buying at any one time. He almost *never* gives anyone a hint of where his interests lie. But at the same time, Buffett has always been aware that there are other investors doing the same thing he is doing—scenting out the terrain carefully.

Investment writers have called his type of sniffing around "coattailing"—that is, riding on the coattails of successful investors. The trick, of course, is not to tip your hand at all when you have discovered something that is of interest to you, and to move in quickly and buy up as much as you can before the coattailers do the same thing.

That brings up a warning that Buffett is well aware of:

"For some reason, people take their cues from price action rather than from values. What doesn't work is when you start doing things that you don't understand or because they worked last week for somebody else. The dumbest reason in the world to buy a stock is because it's going up."

And that usually happens when a number of people begin picking away at one certain stock. As soon as the demand becomes evident, the price rises automatically. The secret of true coattailing is the timing. One nanosecond late, and your big find is history.

The point must be made here that Warren Buffett does not depend at all on coattailing in its accepted sense. He would never try to ride on the coattails of someone else. The reason is an obvious one. He has already been there. He has read all the facts he can about the company and formed his opinion by the time there are any coattailers in sight.

It is something for the tyro investor to think about.

VII. The Secret of Compound Interest

The real secret of making money in investment is a mathematical one: compounding interest. For example, if a person puts $2,000 into an IRA account when he or she is nineteen and continues investing $2,000 a year for eight years more, until twenty-seven, then when he or she retires at sixty-five, the original stake of $18,000 will have grown to over a million dollars.

Of course this equation makes the basic assumption that the money will be working at 10 percent per annum compounded—and that's a pretty easy assumption to make. It was just such "compounding" of interest that made Buffett a millionaire at such an early age. Then again, he did start earlier than the age of nineteen.

Value investing is based on the compounding of interest. The secret of this particular factor is to keep the money where it is and let it work steadily toward the goal you have in mind. The good years don't matter all that much; they help cancel out the bad years that are bound to occur no matter what kind of gyrations the market is going through.

The idea, in baseball terms, is to work for a high and consistent batting average, and not to sweat out the home runs.

About earnings generally, Buffett had this to say:

"We like stocks that generate high returns on invested capital where there is a strong likelihood that [the stock] will continue to do so. For example, the last time we bought Coca-Cola, it was selling at about 23 times earnings. Using our purchase price and today's earnings, that makes it about 5 times earnings. It's really the interaction of capital employed, the return on that capital, and the future capital generated versus the purchase price today."

VIII. Know When to Invest

The eighth key element in successful investment involves gyrations of the stock market. Actually, the best time to buy, as any fool knows, is when stocks are low in price. Stocks go down when there has been a reverse in the market—that is, when the average drops. Most of the stocks drop with the average.

The idea is a simple one. Wait for the market to collapse, then go in and buy up. Waiting for a collapse may seem an endless process, but eventual collapses or downturns are inevitable. The idea is to get in and buy when everybody else is selling off because of a downturn that scares them.

"We have no idea how long the excesses will last," Buffett once said, referring to the actions of the market in March 1989, when the numbers soared. "Nor do we know what will change the attitudes of the government, lender, and buyer that fuel them. But we know that the less prudence with which others conduct their affairs, the greater the prudence with which we should conduct our own affairs."

IX. Never Run with the Street Pack

Number nine is actually a negative position: it's what *not* to do to be a good investor. And Warren Buffett has made his name pointing out the foibles and the futilities of would-be investors who thought they knew what they were doing—but didn't.

Here's something to remember always:

"Risk comes from not knowing what you are doing."

Investors have a habit of checking out their pet theories on friends. And this means that they are instinctively seeking some kind of recommendation from their broker friends. Buffett has a good homespun Nebraska aphorism for that situation:

"Never ask the barber if you need a haircut."

Buffett has always had a good fix on money managers and professionals who advise investors what stocks and what bonds to invest in.

"Full-time professionals in other fields, let's say dentists, bring a lot to the layman. But in aggregate, people get nothing for their money from professional money managers."

Another of Buffett's warnings about Wall Street "wizards" of finance goes like this:

"It has always been a fantasy of mine that a boatload of 25 brokers would be shipwrecked and struggle to an island from which there could be no rescue. Faced with developing an economy that would maximize their consumption and pleasure, would they, I wonder, assign 20 of their number to produce food, clothing, shelter, etc., while setting five to trading options endlessly on the future output of the 20?"

As for the average investor in his day-to-day dealings in the marketplace, Buffett has these words of caution and warning:

"The market, like the Lord, helps those who help themselves. But, unlike the Lord, the market does not forgive those who know not what they do."

Words to live by.

INDEX

ABOUT THE AUTHOR

JAY STEELE is a well-known New York author. He has written more than thirty-five books on a wide variety of subjects and was the editor of *The Wall Street Reader*.